ADVANC

"Imagine the power of tens of millions of people suddenly having the time and flexibility to adopt, to foster, to build homes and community centers for the marginalized, to speak to someone who is hurting, to move back home, to care for their aging parents. To change the world one heart at a time. Imagine 'I can't because of my commute/schedule/location' not being a thing. This is why remote matters. This is why this book matters."
　　　　—DARREN MURPH, Head of Remote at GitLab

"When it comes to remote work, Jordan walks the talk. He's lived the remote lifestyle, and in every coaching moment, he intimately understands what these companies are looking for and how professionals can best position themselves to integrate their work and lifestyle."
　　　　—MADELINE MANN, Founder of Self Made Millennial

"There's a very small number of people at the center of the remote work movement like Jordan is. Asking why he's qualified to write this book is like debating whether or not Michael Jordan should take the last shot of the game."
　　　　—CHASE WARRINGTON, Head of Remote at Doist

"A lot of individuals who haven't had the opportunity to work a flexible role don't really have a starting point. They are more or less tied to the mandates of their employer, and they need a resource like Remote for Life to help them better understand how to achieve their goals."
　　　　—TARA VASDANI, Founder of Remote Law Canada

"Jordan has been working with different people from different countries for a long time. He's able to use that perspective to codify the themes and create a template for those looking for all different types of jobs who share the values of autonomy, freedom, and diverse perspective."

—DARCY BOLES, future of work thought leader
and remote work consultant

"I speak at remote work conferences all over the world, and Jordan Carroll's tactics and methods for helping people land their remote dream job are the best I've seen. Plus, he's done it himself. He is a walking case study of exactly what works today in our rapidly changing society."

—MATT BOWLES, Host of *The Maverick Show* podcast

"Finding your dream job isn't about the job; it's about finding the dream you. Jordan thinks by the minute about creating the best version of himself, and when he works with his clients, you can see his passion for bringing out their best."

—DANNY PAGE, VP of Operations at Enduring Technologies

"As a digital nomad community builder, remote work influencer, and friend of Jordan, his book is a must-read for anyone looking to tap into their own ideal lifestyle by taking advantage of the global remote work movement."

—OLÚMIDÉ GBENRO, digital nomad community builder

REMOTE FOR LIFE

REMOTE FOR LIFE

How to Find a Flexible Job and
Fast Forward to Freedom

JORDAN CARROLL

Hardcover ISBN: 978-1-5445-3678-1
Paperback ISBN: 978-1-5445-3679-8
Ebook ISBN: 978-1-5445-3680-4

To my immediate family: my mother, father, sister, aunt, and late grandparents, this book wouldn't have been possible without your support and encouragement.

To my extended family: those who passed before they could see me write this, and also those who risked everything to come to America generations ago to escape famines in Wales, I'm indebted to your decision to create a better life.

To my best friend Danny Orchard, who left us far too soon, I dedicate this book to you, my friend. Your spirit lives on and guides my intuitive decisions every, single, day.

To my past, current, and future clients, to those who've watched my videos, engaged with my content, or followed my work—without being able to serve you, this means nothing.

Thank you all.

I hope you enjoy this book as much as I enjoyed finally getting this shit done.

CONTENTS

FOREWORD

REMOTE WORK IS *DEEPLY PERSONAL* TO ME.

I value geographic flexibility and workplace autonomy over the usual suspects of salary, title, and fame. Working remotely has fundamentally shaped the fabric of my family.

I've spent my entire career working across the spectrum of remote, with more than fifteen years leading remote teams and charting remote transformations. I advise and invest in global startups and serve as a remote work transformation consultant. I serve multifaceted teams across people, operations, and marketing functions.

I'm currently GitLab's Head of Remote. GitLab is one of the world's largest all-remote companies, with more than 1,500 team members spread across sixty-seven countries, with no company-owned offices.

I first met Jordan Carroll when he was interviewing me for his show, *Remote Weekly Spotlight*. We had an incredibly vulnerable, public conversation about why remote matters. We went well beyond the usual topics of productivity and culture. The heart of remote work is something much deeper.

It's about much more than an altered workspace. It's about an altered *life*, and life itself is the focus.

Remote work allows for sharing and exploration. It enabled me to achieve a Guinness World Record in publishing, to fly more than 1.2 million miles (equivalent to flying to the moon five times), and to pursue hobbies in aviation, music, photography, and more.

Most important of all, as an adoptive father (my life's greatest achievement), it keeps me near family and community. Our adoption would not have happened without the flexibility remote work affords.

It is my goal to enable ever more people to free themselves from a daily commute and to do work that fulfills their soul. I believe remote work can reverse rural depopulation, make communities less transitory, and spread opportunities to underserved areas.

Decoupling society from the rigidity of a commute enables people to contribute much more to the world. It empowers people to be present for others who need their time and attention outside of work.

Imagine the power of tens of millions of people suddenly having the time and flexibility to adopt, to foster, to build homes and community centers for the marginalized, to speak to someone who is hurting, to move back home, to care for their aging parents. To change the world one heart at a time.

Imagine "I can't, because of my commute/schedule/location" not being a thing.

This is why remote matters.

This is why this book matters.

—DARREN MURPH,
Head of Remote at GitLab
Guinness World Record–holding journalist
Author of *Living the Remote Dream*
World Traveler and Adoptive Father

INTRODUCTION

YOU PICKED UP THIS BOOK FOR A REASON. I DON'T KNOW THE REASON, but I can take a few guesses.

You feel trapped. If you're living that cubicle life, each day you wake up in a box, get in a box with wheels, and then spend all day working in another box. You know you're stuck in a rut, and if something doesn't change, you'll spend your whole life this way, only to one day die and be carried out of this world in…yet another box. I've got nothing against boxes, but that's undeniably depressing.

Or maybe your coworker Steve, who has the personality of a dishrag, eats lunch at his desk every day and he's got some weird, insatiable appetite for canned tuna. Not only that, but if you have to listen to him chew with his mouth open one more time, you're going to lose your shit. Honestly, anyone who brings fish to an office should be fired.

Perhaps your workplace is toxic, and you're sick of the politics and overwhelming workload. You come home each day feeling drained, stressed, and burned out. Hobbies? Exercise? Friendships? Personal development? You want these things, but where are you supposed to find the energy? The very foundations of a happy and healthy life seem to always be just out of reach. The most you can muster after a long day is vegging out on the couch and flipping through endless options on Netflix, often spending more time clicking the up and down buttons on the remote than actually watching something.

You might be a parent wanting more time with your children. Whether you've taken inspiration from those who worldschool their kids while traveling (my friend Ken Weary does this), or you just want to be as present as possible for all the firsts—first word, first steps, first tooth—and for all the seconds, thirds, and fourths too. You want to be there for everything, even when those moments are disgusting, like when they decide that snails are just as much a delicacy straight from the sidewalk as they are as hors d'oeuvres in France. Speaking from experience, I had a quite refined palate at an early age.

Maybe you were given the opportunity to work from home because of COVID-19, and like one of those viral videos where a color-blind child puts on special glasses for the first time, you finally see the beauty you've been missing. You're much more productive without constant interruptions and distractions. Now your company is requiring you to come back into the office, and the thought of smelling Steve's tuna again makes you gag.

Perhaps you're currently working remotely, but the job or company isn't the right fit. Maybe you want a position that gives you increased autonomy over your schedule, more challenge and upward mobility, or will actually let you travel outside of your city or state. Maybe you've always wanted to see the world, and hope one day you can find a position that allows you to live the digital nomad lifestyle, gallivanting from country to country each month.

Or you could be a new grad in the early stages of your career, feeling discouraged that most companies seem to require multiple years of experience and wishing a company would give you a shot at a legitimate entry-level remote role.

I don't know your specific reasons for picking up this book, but I know this: If you want more freedom in your life, it's time for you to think outside the box. The good thing is, this is the best time in history to make it happen, and you're not alone.

The Remote Revolution

I started writing this book in 2018, and I'm glad I didn't finish it. It would have been awkward two years later when the COVID-19 pandemic swept across the world. For once, procrastination actually paid off. The job marketplace has been moving toward flexible work for years, but the pandemic accelerated these changes to a whole new level.

Mandatory shutdowns completely disrupted the workplace. Companies that previously scoffed at remote work had to make a choice: embrace remote work or go out of business. Forced to adapt, many businesses—and employees—soon discovered remote work was not only possible, but advantageous.

I immediately knew we were on the edge of something big: a remote revolution. After having the opportunity to work remotely and experience all the associated freedom, people wouldn't want to return to the office. To me it's obvious: *Of course,* people want to keep working remotely. *Of course,* they want more freedom, not less.

The remote revolution is officially here, which creates both challenges and opportunities for you, depending on how you look at it. The opportunity? More companies than ever are offering remote positions. The challenge? More people than ever want to work remotely, creating absurd levels of competition for even basic work-from-home jobs. If you've spent any time looking for a remote job, you've likely run into at least one of these problems:

- You struggle to find legitimate, well-paying remote opportunities, though you've seen plenty of ridiculous claims about how you can make $5,000/week working from home filling out surveys, with no experience necessary! (Run far, far away.)

- You're underqualified for most of the remote job postings you find and wonder why the hell all these entry-level jobs require three to five years of experience.

- You feel overqualified for the remote job postings you're finding and feel like you're going to have to settle for way less than you deserve.

- You send out dozens, even hundreds of applications and résumés without getting any responses, leaving you feeling dejected and discouraged.

- When you do make it to the interview phase, you struggle to articulate your value and can't seem to get over the final hurdle to land the job.

- Where you're from or where you currently live is an obstacle since so many remote jobs have geographical restrictions.

With all these roadblocks, it's easy to get frustrated and overwhelmed. You might lose confidence in your abilities and even feel like giving up. But the reality is, being good at your job and being good at the job search are two different skill sets. Most people suck at searching for a remote job because chances are, they've never been taught how to do it! Beating yourself up over this is like criticizing a sixteen-year-old for a bad merge on the freeway during their first driving class. But luckily for you, job searching doesn't entail potential catastrophic injury because you didn't check your blind spot.

I want you to think back to all the jobs you've had in life. How did you land them? What are the patterns you can identify? Would Bob Ross look at your experience on your résumé and say, "Look at all these happy accidents?" Do you feel like you could repeat your results and find a remote job you love that gives you the flexibility your lifestyle requires?

If not, this book is for you. If you've never been taught how to land a remote job, this book is for you. If you know you need some guidance in this process, this book is for you.

My goal is to help you create a system for searching, finding, and getting hired by remote companies, as well as to identify the types of remote companies that will allow you to live your ideal lifestyle. It's to give you something you can use the rest of your life to help not only improve your chances of success, but to create consistent predictability of results. To give you a flow of inbound opportunities instead of constantly applying online without getting responses. To give you a real strategy, because without one, how could you expect your situation to get any better?

Why I Wrote This Book

I found my first remote job on Craigslist as a telemarketer in 2013. Surprising, I know, that you could use black market eBay for anything other than awkward encounters with sociopaths. (Side note: There are much better places to find remote jobs now than Craigslist. I wouldn't recommend it unless you enjoy the thrill of potentially being turned into a lampshade. I digress.)

Being a remote telemarketer in 2013 was about as glorious as it seems. I would squeeze hour-long "call-blitzes" in between a full-time university course load and two other part-time jobs. Little did I know, the remote work movement would become the most impactful cultural phenomenon in my life moving forward.

Since that time, I've worked remotely across a wide variety of industries, companies, and roles. I've held remote positions with a global Fortune 50 tech company with more than 400,000 employees (IBM); a fully distributed, remote-first travel company with 150 employees (Remote Year); and startups ranging from 2 to 50 employees. I've worked for others, freelanced, and run my own businesses. While working remotely I've lived all over the world—in the United States (where I'm from), Mexico (where I also have residency), and over a dozen other countries.

I've been in the trenches, and these experiences have given me a unique and valuable perspective. I realized that there's a learning curve to finding remote work, articulating your value as a candidate, and actually becoming a high-performing remote worker. These aren't subjects taught in school! But hey, at least I remember how to do long division and know what an isosceles triangle is, right? (Spoiler: I can't, and I don't.)

At some point in my journey between 2016 and 2018, I started getting a lot of questions. Questions from folks like yourself, asking about how to find remote work. Thus, the Remote Job Coach alter ego, or persona, or whatever the hell you want to call it, was born. And I set out to educate others. I distilled my experiences into timeless lessons and a proven system for how to get hired to work remotely.

Clients I've worked with who weren't getting responses from hundreds of applications used this process to get a job without even applying. Others who were terrified of networking on LinkedIn used my templates to confidently send out dozens of messages a week and make valuable connections with ease. Some clients who never got past the first round of interviews finally internalized their value, prepared their stories efficiently, and began wowing interviewers.

In this book, you'll come across many case studies of my clients. My hope is that you can see yourself in some of these examples, and it can provide you motivation to keep going. I will never be the person to tell you that you can't do something. But know this: it will take work. It's up to you, and there's no magic pill. Here's what a few of my clients have said about their results to get you hyped:

- **Esther:** "The skills and strategies I learned from Jordan are not just for the job search, they are lifelong skills that will continue to benefit me for years to come."

- **Lauren:** "The biggest transformation for me when I search for jobs was being able to focus step-by-step instead of looking at the whole big picture, which was overwhelming."

- **Nicholas:** "When I was doing it on my own, I was really focused on job boards, finding a job listed on there and submitting an application. After working with Jordan, it changed my approach to networking first. I didn't even have to submit applications for a lot of the jobs I ended up interviewing for."

- **Nicole:** "The biggest transformation for me looking for remote work was the effort I would put into each job itself. It came from not just putting my résumé out there, but doing more research into who was hiring, how to contact them, how to further make connections with them and build a network that would actually support me."

- **Katelyn:** "I only ended up applying for two jobs and was able to land one of those with a referral."

The strategies illustrated in my content, courses, and coaching programs have reached hundreds of thousands of individuals (hopefully millions by the time you're reading this!). Many of them have used the methodologies to improve their job search. Nothing fills me with a greater sense of purpose than a random message from a job seeker telling me they landed a remote position because of my advice.

Now, with this book, I hope to help even more people—and eventually get one of those messages from you.

Remote Work Saved My Life

After receiving my bachelor's in business administration and marketing, I landed a well-paying corporate sales opportunity with IBM in

Somerville, Massachusetts. I was the first student from my school to be offered a position in IBM's training program, and I felt a huge sense of pride. I had done everything society told me to do: went to college, graduated, and got a corporate job. Being able to move right outside of Boston was also a new and exciting experience, as I grew up a Boston sports fan (my extended family is from there and brainwashed me at a young age).

So why wasn't I happy?

There were lots of things I could blame it on. It was the coldest and snowiest season in the past decade; quite a feat for a New England winter to outdo itself. Being from California, I was way out of my element. And oh, man, the commute was a bitch—upwards of 1.5 hours each way. It was excruciating, especially in the winter.

My days in the office could be brutal too. See, my training program gave me more opportunity and upward mobility much faster than many of my senior colleagues, which led to resentment. I felt uncomfortable with the politics, the side-eyes in the hallways, and overall disdain for my existence. I imagine if I'd worked at a company for a decade and some snot-nosed kid out of college was set to pass my pay band in a year or two, I would be upset too.

I felt unfulfilled and sad all the time. Part of that was owed to the soul-crushing fact that my entire days were consumed by working and commuting, and there wasn't much room left for *living*. But if I'm being honest, I can't blame my unhappiness on my job. Looking back at this time of my life, there were deeper issues at play that require a *rewind*.

While I'd say my upbringing was pretty good—I had two loving parents and anything I could ever need growing up—none of us escaped childhood without trauma. I grew up overweight, bullied, and feeling outcasted.

Food was always my go-to comfort, and eventually, my escape upgraded to drugs and alcohol. In high school, the majority of my friends were made through our common desire to smoke a blunt before class. I was always anxious, especially socially. The weed definitely didn't help with that. A constant case of the "munchies" kept me in a rotation of Taco Bell and Jack in the Box drive-thrus, which only contributed to my insecurity about my weight.

In college, I redefined myself, but not necessarily in a good way. I found I could escape my anxiety and insecurity by drinking copious amounts of alcohol.

In solving one problem, I created countless new ones. For those who've never blacked out before, it's not something I'd advise trying for fun. I got into fights for no reason, was admitted to the hospital twice, woke up in jail on three separate occasions, and consumed hard drugs I don't remember doing, all as the result of my decisions after "just one more drink."

Not only did I damage relationships, embarrass myself, and spend *way* too much money, but I put myself and others in compromising situations. I lost cell phones, wallets, keys, and even my fucking *shoes*. I once walked barefoot and shirtless for three miles on the side of a highway after losing my phone and wallet after a July 4th party in Lake Tahoe.

I didn't question my behavior because it seemed like "everyone was doing it." There was some truth in that, but it's a terrible excuse.

The truth is: I was so fucking lost.

I built up so much shame, resentment, and hatred toward myself. In some of my darkest spirals of depression and anxiety, I thought about how killing myself would be so much easier than continuing. I never took action on those thoughts, but it scared me that my mind could go there.

Fast forward.

Even with the personal issues I've outlined, it has always been important to me to do well in life. I maintained high marks in school, was heavily involved in clubs on campus, and at one point held three part-time jobs at once. That pattern continued at IBM. From an outside perspective, I was successful, but I had low self-esteem and continued to mask my emotions and escape them at every opportunity with food and alcohol. I'd go on weekend-long benders, getting hammered and eating pizza. It's like I was living a double life. Work hard, play hard, I guess?

If that wasn't enough, I also felt a deeper, existential crisis about not making a difference in the world. At times, it felt like I was trapped, and nothing would ever change. Then I had the opportunity to work remotely. It's not like that immediately fixed all my problems, but I credit remote work with empowering me to get through difficult times. On days where my personal demons were the loudest, I know being stuck in an office would have made it much worse.

Remote work fundamentally changed what was possible for me in my lifestyle, health, and relationships. It allowed me to build work around travel: inhabiting dozens of different countries while working and ultimately becoming a resident of Mexico. It gave me time to pursue hobbies like video production, Spanish, and stand-up comedy. It gave me the flexibility to prioritize health. As I built a more fulfilling life, I didn't feel the same need to escape, at least not in the ways I did previously. Because of that, I quit many of the substances that I previously used as numbing agents, including cigarettes, alcohol, and drugs (except natural psychedelics and, well, caffeine, of course). From my heaviest point, I lost forty pounds and 15% body fat in ninety days and started competing in Spartan Races, Tough Mudders, and international marathons.

My career priority shifted to finding more meaningful work. I sought out small start-ups where I could have more impact, including working for a dating coach, a PR firm, and a travel/experience company. I freelanced as an outbound sales rep for hire, content marketer, and B2B tech writer. For as different as my jobs and gigs were, a common thread pulls them all together: remote work and the strategies I used to secure them.

Eventually, I started my own businesses focused on guiding others to find more freedom and flexibility in their lives. I've been able to use my knowledge and resources to work toward my greater purpose of helping those for whom remote work can be the biggest lifesaver: underprivileged populations, those with disabilities, and refugees. I donate time and 10% of all my business's profits to various causes that support that mission (including the money made from this book, so thank you for helping the world!).

Ultimately, I'm the one who made the changes that turned my life around. I decided to quit drinking. I decided to eat better and prioritize my mental and physical fitness. I decided to pursue new career opportunities. But it was remote work that gave me the freedom to make those choices.

Today, I'm still in the process of growing and building the life I want, which is a never-ending journey. But being "Remote for Life" means thanks to remote work, my choices are endless. Remote work is about so much more than wearing sweats to work or taking a nap in the middle of the day. It's about *autonomy*—the ability to decide who you want to be and how you're going to show up in the world. That's what remote work gave to me, and I want to give you a Remote for your life, too.

Grab the Remote Control

In this book, my goal is not to show you how to live my life, but to teach you how to secure remote work opportunities so you can create your *own* ideal life of freedom. You'll learn clear, tangible steps to help you wherever you're at in your remote work journey. While I mention some specific tools and apps, I try to keep the information as evergreen as possible, with the intention for it to be relevant decades from now. With as fast as the world is changing, we can both admit that's an idealistic vision. You'll learn:

- The realities of remote work—the good, bad, and ugly (but mostly good)

- The importance of creating a vision, so you can work toward *your* dream life, not someone else's

- The right mindset that will give you the confidence and resiliency to succeed

- How to actually get shit done as a remote worker and become the type of employee companies want to hire

- How to leverage your current skills (because you're probably more qualified than you think) and build new ones if needed

- Tips on branding yourself to stand out from the crowd and make employers come to you

- Strategies to effectively network (even for introverts), unlocking secret back doors into remote opportunities

- How to find legitimate, well-paying remote positions (they *do* exist!)

- Ways to make sure your application doesn't immediately end up in the trash (like most applications do) and get responses instead of being ghosted

- How to articulate your value, internalize your stories, and nail your interviews

- Tips and strategies for working abroad, so it's more than a glorified vacation

By implementing the strategies I teach, you'll never have to go back to the office (unless you want to) and you'll be able to use the freedom of remote work to improve your life. Throughout this book, my goal is to equip you with the tactics that help you land a flexible position. To that end, I've included many exercises. To get the most out of them, I recommend completing them as you read. I've also created extra resources to dive deeper into topics that extend beyond the scope of this book.

I gathered all the exercises and resources, along with an up-to-date list of recommended tools, into a resource library available at www. theremotejobcoach.com/book-resources. Bookmark this link now, because you'll come back to it a lot.

With some education and work, you can gain the metaphorical "remote control" to start living the life of your dreams. We weren't meant to cram our lives into boxes. You can have both a successful career and a fulfilling personal life. It's time to think outside the box and fast-forward to freedom. Let's press the power button and get started.

CHAPTER 1

MUTE THE NOISE

Debunking Remote Work Misconceptions

THE REMOTE REVOLUTION—WHAT SHOULD BE AN EXCITING TIME FOR all—is still met with skepticism and doubt by many. While remote work is clearly here to stay, it doesn't help that heaps of companies who went remote during the pandemic are constantly threatening to "pull the rug" and go back to the office.

Reed Hastings, the co-founder of Netflix, told the *Wall Street Journal*, "Not being able to get together in person, particularly internationally, is a pure negative," and that Netflix would be back in the office as soon as possible.

Goldman Sachs CEO David Solomon said about remote work, "This is not ideal for us and it's not a new normal. It's an aberration that we are going to correct as quickly as possible."

At the time of me writing this, neither company is fully back in an office setting. And, I imagine if they do fully go back, they'll encounter resistance from employees and many will leave for companies offering more flexibility. An estimated one in two people won't return to jobs that don't offer remote work post-pandemic, according to a 2020 study by Owl Labs.

For every company pushing a desperate return to the office, there are companies who've seen the writing on the wall and embraced their "remote work experiment." Corporations like Square, Quora, Coinbase, Dropbox, Slack, Spotify, Twitter, and many more made announcements during the pandemic that they were permanently incorporating remote work into their organizational strategy.

Not only that, but the statistics are clear:

- Remote job searching itself is increasing, per Glassdoor, as people looking for remote work through search grew 360% between June 2019 and June 2021.

- Job listings for remote work are up. From 2020 to 2021, LinkedIn saw an increase of 357% in job postings offering "remote work," and the number is continuing to rise.

- Remote workers are getting paid better. According to Owl Labs' study, 2020 saw a 65% increase in remote workers making over $100k in 2020.

- People want the choice of remote work! Per Buffer, 99% of people would choose to work remotely for the rest of their life, even if it was just part-time.

- Companies are accepting remote work. By 2028, 73% of all departments are expected to have remote workers according to Upwork.

The reality is, the companies who are shrugging off remote work will be the ones struggling to retain talent. The best employees will demand flexibility, and they'll go wherever they feel valued and trusted. Companies that don't have a remote strategy will also incur more costs, and over the coming decades, remote work will be the norm, not the exception.

Even with all this anecdotal and statistical evidence, I still receive messages weekly from job seekers who don't think they'll be able to work remotely. I talk to some who are working remotely now but don't see any upward mobility or challenge in their current role. Some want to start traveling but their company has geographical restrictions in their remote policy, and it's preventing them from living their dream.

There's a lot of noise surrounding remote work—from myths to blatant falsehoods. Wherever you're at in this process, before making your next leap, let's mute the noise and debunk some common misconceptions.

Misconception #1: Remote Working Is a Fad

Due to the COVID-19 pandemic, in the span of weeks, remote work went from a nice-to-have perk to an absolute necessity if you wanted to survive as a business. Soon, you couldn't spend a day online without another recorded Zoom call going viral because someone left their camera on while taking a shit.

Yet many have chalked remote work up as a fad—a product of the COVID-19 pandemic that will slowly fade out of public consciousness once it's no longer necessary, joining the likes of the Harlem Shake, Pokémon Go, and eating Tide Pods. I mean, if you're still eating Tide Pods now, come on, that's so 2017. In other words, once the pandemic is "over," we'll go back to "normal."

But the pandemic didn't *invent* remote work. Remote work existed long before.

As early as 1979, Frank Schiff wrote an article in the *Washington Post* titled "Working at Home Can Save Gasoline." Throughout the '80s, companies like JCPenney, American Express, The Hartford, GE, and Levi Strauss implemented telecommuting programs for employees. In 1987, the *Christian Science Monitor* claimed about 1.5 million Americans were telecommuters and 300 companies ran telecommuting programs. Eventually, this "perk" started becoming a valid business strategy. Fast-forward and you'll find an organization like Automattic, the company that founded WordPress, has been globally distributed since its inception in 2005 (now with 1,800+ employees in almost 100 countries). Even stats from the National Telecommunications and Information Administration right before the pandemic indicate that in 2019, approximately 51 million Americans reported using the internet to work remotely. COVID simply amplified and accelerated a trend already in motion.

As a result, we're seeing more and more *remote-first* companies—businesses that are founded with cultures intentionally built for remote work. The pandemic provided proof of concept on a larger scale. We now *know* remote work is a viable option for more industries and jobs than many expected. We also know, in the worst-case scenario, remote work could be a necessity. Considering this, it makes sense to build our work around flexibility rather than around an office. Remote work is becoming the default option.

Even among companies built around an *office-first* culture, we're likely to see an adaptable approach moving into the future. Some roles will be performed in the office, some will be performed remotely, and some may be a combination of the two, with certain days or hours in the office and some at home.

Remote work will be more than a fad for the simple reason that it makes business sense. What's the one thing every business loves? Money. According to Global Workplace Analytics, a typical US employer can save an average of $11,000 per employee with remote work in place. And if it's done the right way, it leads to happier and more engaged employees, which are more productive employees. More productivity equals, guess what? More money.

And it's not just about money. It's also about talent. With remote work, businesses can draw from a much wider pool of talent. Their options are no longer limited to those people who live within commuting distance (or who are willing to relocate within commuting distance). Depending on the company's policies, now they can hire people from *all over the state, the country, or possibly even the world.* In a study by Growmotely in 2020, 97% of respondents don't want to return to the office full-time. The top talent in the world expects flexibility, so if companies want the best of the best, that's what they'll need to offer to stay competitive.

Still not convinced remote work is here to stay? Consider climate change. According to the EPA, remote workers in the USA avoid emitting 3.6 million tons of greenhouse gases every year, which is equivalent to planting 91 million trees. As the effects of climate change worsen, remote work will become more necessary than ever.

Remote work is not just the future; it's the now, and it's here to stay.

Misconception #2: All Remote Work Is the Same

Not all remote jobs are created equal. According to research from FlexJobs, due to tax laws and other legalities, 95% of remote jobs have some sort of restriction: time zone, geographic area, country, and so on. While this challenge created a market for global HR software companies like Remote, Oyster, and Deel (which help businesses stay compliant while hiring internationally), a large majority of companies still have restrictions on who and where they hire. Some partial remote positions even require you to visit the office occasionally.

It can be an incredibly frustrating scenario to do all the work of researching and applying to a position, only to discover it doesn't actually offer the level of remote that you desire. And this isn't always easily found on a job listing. I once had a client who made it to a second-round interview with a company that had advertised a "US - Remote" position.

Typically, this would indicate that an employee could live anywhere in the United States. However, in that interview, they asked her if she was willing to relocate because their plan was to go back to the office. She was taken aback and dropped out of the process.

The issue is systemic. Hiring websites and job boards sometimes use different jargon, companies don't have firm remote policies (especially in the flux of the pandemic), and job seekers are often left confused about what to believe.

Going forward, I think it will be mandatory that companies become more transparent about their intentions. I think hiring sites will add more consistent language and customization that allow companies to articulate their intentions in a complete way. But human error will always be part of the process. Those hiring will sometimes misclassify or misstate their remote work classification.

While I try to give people the benefit of the doubt as much as possible, when a company makes an error like that in a job description, it poses a huge red flag. If they can't get it right in their marketing to candidates, can you imagine how confusing it must be to work there? Until there's more standardization around the terminology of remote work, it's important for you to know that not all remote work is the same. It benefits you immensely to be able to distinguish companies that believe in remote work as part of their ethos versus those that are "remote by accident."

In this book, I'll be using terms and phrases about remote work that you may or may not be familiar with. The important part is that we're on the same page, using the same definitions. There are a variety of ways that experts and laymen describe these concepts and there's so much damn nuance required when explaining them, so stick with me.

Before we get into the company models and other levels of remote work roles, let's take a second to clarify the term "remote work" in general.

In its simplest form, remote work means not working from a *centralized* office. It's an umbrella term that can be used to describe a range of situations. When someone works from home, that's remote work. When someone can work from anywhere and travels as a digital nomad, that's considered remote work. When someone works out of their favorite local café, that's remote work. Even if someone goes into a coworking space, but their team isn't centralized in that office, it's considered remote work.

It's helpful to get clarification, especially from companies you're interested in working for, as to exactly what their version of "remote" actually means.

TYPICAL REMOTE WORK MODELS FOR COMPANIES

Companies have different remote work policies, based on numerous factors: tax laws, regulations, location of incorporation, leadership experience, and much more.

- **All-Remote/Fully Distributed**—At these companies, everyone works remotely, 100% of the time, and they can "Work from Anywhere." These companies have the fewest hiring restrictions, usually boasting a globally distributed workforce and no centralized office.

- **Remote-First**—These organizations lead with remote work policy at the forefront of their culture. They are supportive and encouraging of remote work, and even if they have offices, they don't centralize operations there. They might not be remote 100% of the time, but they design policies and workflows like they are.

- **Remote Okay/Friendly**—In this case, a company may allow its employees to work remotely as a choice, but with some baggage. There's a distinction between being okay with remote work and being remote-first. This is the difference between *allowing* and *supporting.* In these companies, the infrastructure to promote great remote work collaboration isn't quite there, and employees may be left feeling less than valued.

- **Remote by Accident**—These companies were not designed to support remote work but fell into it by accident, as a necessity of circumstances, like what happened during the COVID-19 pandemic. As a job seeker, be wary of such companies. When organizations go into business without thinking about their remote work policy and the legal implications involved, it's difficult to retroactively recreate that part of the culture. These are also the companies that might do a "rug pull" and bring people back to the office.

- **Hybrid**—In hybrid-remote environments, some employees work from home, while others go into the office. Using GitLab's terms, this is a "tempting compromise that masks many downsides." The administrative burden of operating two core employee experiences (office vs. remote) makes managing people more difficult, causes rifts and jealousy between employees, and creates confusing hiring practices (i.e., who is remote vs. who isn't?).

- **Office-Centric/No Remote**—Businesses that don't allow any type of remote work. Either the business model itself is incongruent with remote work, or leadership is biased toward working in a centralized office. The ironic part about this model is that "multinational corporations with multiple offices across the globe are inherently remote, even if they do not allow remote work." Not recognizing that can cause difficulty when teams collaborate across these different time zones and locations. I have GitLab and Darren to thank for all the mic drop moments they provided me in this section.

REMOTE WORK LEVELS FOR JOB ROLES

Regardless of a company's work model, carefully read job listings to evaluate what type of restrictions might apply to a specific role. For example, you may find an all-remote company that's hiring a customer support rep to respond to requests in APAC (Asia-Pacific). Even though the company is set up to hire from anywhere, since the role is time zone-dependent, they'll likely only consider candidates within that time zone. The phrases below describe the level of remote for a specific job.

- **100% Remote Work**—The role in question has no requirement to be in an office. However, it may still be restricted by location, so it's important to double-check.

- **Temporarily Remote**—This is the murky water you'd rather not wade in. The company intends on bringing this role back to an office at some point.

- **Hybrid Remote Work**—Hybrid indicates you'll work some time in an office and sometimes remote, usually working from home.

- **Option for Remote Work**—I would call this akin to "remote-friendly." Remote is an option, but probably not supported as much as you'll find in a 100% remote role.

- **Office-Based**—I hope I don't need to explain this one.

TYPES OF REMOTE WORKERS

There are various ways to work remotely as an individual. The true beauty of remote work is choice!

- **Remote employees**—Remote employees work for a company full-time as "in-house staff." They may receive benefits, depending on the company's policies, and often work for a regular wage or salary. Employees are expected to be hired long-term, and taxes automatically come out of the paychecks they receive.

- **Remote freelancers**—Also known as independent contractors, freelancers are typically hired on a project basis, and they may have multiple different clients they service at once. Freelancers can work in a more flexible fashion but are responsible for filing their own taxes and dealing with liability. (More on freelancing in chapter 8.)

- **Remote business owners**—These are people who own a location-independent business. In contrast to freelancers, who are selling a skill and often exchange their time for money, business owners focus on creating a business as an asset that can generate revenue with or without them. This route requires a lot of energy and time upfront, but can pay off for those who can stomach the risk and effort required.

- **Digital nomads**—This term actually made it to the Merriam-Webster dictionary, which goes to show how mainstream remote work is becoming. They say, "someone who performs their occupation entirely over the internet while traveling… such a person who has no permanent fixed home address." Digital nomads can be freelancers, remote employees, or business owners, but they have enough freedom in whatever they are doing remotely to be able to travel at the same time. (More on the digital nomad life in chapter 11.)

Ultimately, remote work is highly varied, and all of these options—company work models, job roles, and types of remote workers—have trade-offs. However, when I speak of *true* remote work, I'm referring to 100% remote work that's deployed by remote-first and all-remote/fully distributed companies. *This is the good stuff.* It's focused on trust and flexibility for employees and a commitment to remote work as a competitive advantage for the organization. As you go through this book, keep that in mind.

Misconception #3: You Don't Have a Chance of Getting a Remote Position

I've spoken to many professionals who've never worked remotely before and believe they don't stand a chance of finding a remote position. You may think the same, but your experience and skills are likely more transferable to remote work than you realize.

Though you may not have worked remotely, you've likely worked *virtually*. Remote work is work done away from a centralized office. Virtual work is anything done online. Not all virtual work is remote work, but all remote work includes virtual work. Capiche?

Have you ever emailed coworkers? Participated in videoconferences? Collaborated with a coworker sitting at a different office? That's all virtual work. You may have done it from an office, but you could have as easily done it from somewhere else. Your virtual work experience can translate to remote work.

Just because you lack *direct* experience doesn't mean the door is closed to you. Someone who's worked for a remote company will often have an easier time getting a remote job than someone who hasn't. From what I've seen it often becomes an issue of confidence and belief, more than skill. In chapter 4 we'll go through exercises to evaluate the skills and experience you have to help you understand how they apply to a remote position.

Misconception #4: You Need to Be a _____ or Be in the _____ Industry to Work Remotely

There's also a perception that remote work is only for certain industries or certain types of roles. Many believe remote work is only for the tech industry. Yes, the tech industry lends itself well to remote work, but there are plenty of remote jobs outside of tech. Take one look at FlexJobs' "100 Surprising Jobs" tab and you'll discover remote landscape designers, librarians, teleradiologists, home stylists, prop photographers, tarot card readers, and digital painters.

Hell, even *goats* have remote jobs now. An animal sanctuary in California called Sweet Farm set up a Goat-2-Meeting service where companies can pay to have a goat (or other "animal ambassador") join their video calls to liven things up. And if you're reading this, I assume you're not livestock, and you can be more creative than a farm animal.

My favorite freestyle rapper (and the GOAT), Harry Mack, created a fully sustainable internet income by spittin' rhymes for millions while streaming from the comfort of his home during the pandemic. We are an innovative species. Remember that. So if you're not in tech or another XYZ industry you think of as remote-friendly, don't get discouraged. Look at how many jobs didn't even exist five to ten years ago that are now commonplace. Our society will continue to accelerate in strangeness and utility as remote work becomes more widely accepted.

Another common assumption is that remote work is only for people of a certain age group. Too young, and you don't have enough experience to land a remote position. Too old, and you're not spry enough to manage new technology. I've worked with a wide range of people from age 20 to 70 that have disproved both of those hypotheses.

People may discriminate against you because of your age, but it's always up to you to prove that you can do the work to get the job. Age itself is not the issue. Often the challenge is a lack of experience, lack of digital competency, or inability to articulate one's value.

But these challenges can be overcome. As a coach and someone who's seen all corners of the remote industry, I've been impressed with people's ability to do things they never thought they could do. Ageism is a real thing, but competency speaks the loudest. If you're willing, it's possible to learn the skills to thrive in a remote environment.

Change the Input: Reframe Your Mindset

Your belief systems create your perception of the world.

Whatever beliefs you've held up to this point about finding remote work or your ability to work remotely, it's time to question them. As Henry Ford once said, "Whether you think you can or you can't, you're right."

Misconception #5: There Aren't Any Good Remote Jobs Out There

Another misconception is that there aren't any good, legitimate remote jobs on the market—they're all scams, or they don't have the pay scale and career potential comparable to a traditional job.

Yes, there *are* scams out there, and scammers have gotten creative in tricking people who are desperately looking for work online. (See chapter 6 for a whole section on how to spot and avoid scams.) But there are also plenty of companies, including top-tier Fortune 500 companies, who are offering legitimate opportunities for remote work, with competitive salaries and professional growth opportunities.

For a taste of what's possible in remote work, consider Sacha Connor, a remote work pioneer for the Clorox Company. For eight years, she led large, distributed teams responsible for more than $250 million in sales, with a $25 million marketing budget, and she did it remotely. She was the first fully remote member of the Clorox leadership team, running a $1 billion division, and she paved the way for remote initiatives within the company. Mind you, this was in 2010! Today she's the founder and CEO of Virtual Work Insider, which helps companies work remotely more effectively.

Sacha is not an isolated example. Companies have a lot more resources for remote workers today than they did then. And in terms of salary, the US Census Bureau found the median earnings for people who worked from home in 2018 were about $4,000 higher than the median earnings for all workers.

Misconception #6: *Everything* Is Going to Be Remote

It's an overambitious statement to say that *everything* is going to be remote in the future. Someday maybe, with enough advancements in tech, or after Musk, Zuckerberg, and Bezos microchip all of us with 5G. Or when human genetics merge seamlessly with robotics and we all become cyborgs, that could be true. Perhaps at some point, all of our surgical operations will be done by doctors with remote controls (this is already being done in some places), singers will only put on shows in the metaverse, and robot nannies will know far more about your kids than you do. Hell, I'm reaching here, but part of me wants to reread my book in twenty years and see how many predictions I got right.

The reality today is that not every job is suited for remote work, and even if a job *can* be done remotely—and possibly *was* done remotely, temporarily during the pandemic—many companies are not set up to properly support remote work.

During the pandemic, a wide and surprising array of industries offered remote services. Barbers gave virtual consultations while their clients awkwardly turned their heads toward the camera to get advice on cutting their own cowlicks. Plumbers guided people through pipe repairs over Zoom, probably laughing internally watching them wade through their own sewage. Clothing companies provided virtual fashion consultants and digital "try-on" tools to assist online shoppers, and people's suspicions were confirmed that it looked ugly on them before making a purchase.

These and other examples of remote adoption were innovative solutions for unique circumstances, but they were never meant to be anything more than temporary. A virtual haircut tutorial might prevent me from busting out a bowl and looking like King Curtis from *Wife Swap*, but it's not going to be as good as having a professional do it. Trying on clothing virtually is just not the same as going to a store and putting on a bathing suit that dozens of humans tried on right before me. Oh, and no one actually wants to deal with their own feces when it's not where it should be, so yeah, I'm calling that plumber to come in person.

As a remote job seeker, be aware of the limitations of remote work. Maybe you can do some aspects of your job remotely, but others require you to be on-premises. Perhaps your company offered temporary remote working options but doesn't have the right policies and structure to allow for productive remote work long-term. The better you understand the realities, the better you'll be able to take the steps to achieve what you want—like moving from an office-first culture to a fully remote company or learning new hard skills.

Misconception #7: Remote Work Fixes All Your Problems

Getting a remote job won't automatically fix your issues. Remote work is neither easier nor harder than on-site work. There are challenges to both, and many other factors—like company size, work culture, industry, and role—that will influence your satisfaction with the job.

It's easy to believe that just landing a remote position itself is a source of happiness, but true, lasting happiness has to come internally, not externally. This is something I discovered firsthand. I worked remotely for many years and changed positions and organizations multiple times before finding the kind of work I do today, which gives me a sense of purpose and fulfillment. And as I explained in the introduction, while I credit remote work with saving my life, it was up to me to take advantage of the opportunities it presented me with. Focusing inward and doing the self-work is what actually brought me sustainable internal peace.

Remote work isn't the solution in and of itself; it is a tool to get closer to the life you want.

The Truths of Remote Work

With the misconceptions debunked, let's recap the truths:

- Remote work is here to stay.

- Remote work comes in many forms.

- As long as you're willing to put in the work, a remote job is a possibility for you.

- Remote work is available to all kinds of people, across a wide array of industries.

- There are many legitimate, well-paying remote jobs.

- Many jobs can be done remotely, but not all.

- Remote work isn't a perfect solution; it's a tool to help create the life you want.

Now that you know the facts, let's take a deeper look at what you can expect from remote work—the benefits and the challenges—so you can start visualizing your ideal remote lifestyle.

CHAPTER 2

USE THE CHANNEL GUIDE

Know Your Options

LEXI WAS MISERABLE AT HER NINE-TO-FIVE OFFICE JOB. LIKE SO MANY people interested in remote work, she was looking for a *change*. Within five weeks of us working together, she got it: she received a full-time remote offer for a project management position at an insurance company. It was a new role in a new industry, but she had a friend who worked for the company, and she felt confident she could do it.

She took the job, and she was thrilled…for about a week.

Lexi soon realized many of the company's promises about the job were misaligned with reality. She was working way more hours than expected, and her tasks were repetitive and mundane. This was not what she signed up for. Things had changed all right—but not necessarily for the better.

Shortly before she'd taken the job with the insurance company, Lexi had also scheduled an interview for a social media manager position at a cannabis company. Social media management was her area of expertise and she had previous experience in the cannabis industry. It seemed like a literal perfect fit: work she enjoyed doing, felt passionate about, and had experience in. The only issue? The job started as a part-time position, so while she scheduled the interview, she hadn't considered it a serious option.

Once she received the offer for the insurance job, she asked me if she should cancel the interview with the cannabis company. I encouraged her to take the interview because it was more aligned with her skills and interests, and it would be a good *insurance* policy in case the other job didn't pan out.

She went through with it and received the part-time offer. Originally, her plan was to work both jobs since the cannabis position could be done outside of regular work hours. After only a week and a half of misery at the insurance company, though, the cannabis job turned into a much-needed escape parachute. With this part-time position to fall back on, she yanked the ripcord and quit the insurance job.

After a few months, the cannabis company was so impressed with her performance that they offered her a full-time position. Once again, she was thrilled, but this time, the feeling stayed.

As Lexi learned the hard way, taking a remote job doesn't guarantee happiness or fulfillment. There are as many different types of remote jobs as there are TV channels. Rather than picking a random channel and hoping it's something you want to watch, it's smarter to use the guide. For remote work, a clear vision for what you want and need will guide you to a job that's not only remote but also a good fit for your lifestyle goals.

The Art and Science of Lifestyle Design: What Do You Want?

You're reading this book, so clearly, you want a remote job. Maybe you're miserable in your nine-to-five like Lexi, or you're missing challenge and purpose in your daily life and current role. Maybe you've recently been let go, and you're struggling now to pick up the pieces.

If you just want "something remote," you might end up with something that makes you even more miserable than you are now. Rather than trying to get any remote job, the key is to search for the *right* remote job that enables your ideal remote life.

Lifestyle design is the concept of building the ideal life you want, *now*. The term was initially coined by entrepreneur Tim Ferriss. As he explains in *The 4-Hour Workweek*:

The New Rich (NR) are those who abandon the deferred-life plan and create luxury lifestyles in the present using the currency of the New Rich: time and mobility. This is an art and a science we will refer to as Lifestyle Design (LD).

The traditional life plan is to work for decades in order to save for retirement and finally start living the life you want. Lifestyle design turns that model on its head. Quite frankly, any of us could die tomorrow, so why defer the fun and flexibility for years or decades down the road? Why not design the life you want now instead of putting it on hold until you retire?

Work is not the central focus, your life is; thus, work is made to integrate with your ideal lifestyle rather than the other way around.

Remote work has given more people access to lifestyle design than ever, but it's not a guarantee you'll be able to live the way you want. For instance, a customer service rep might work remotely but still have a strict nine-to-six work schedule where they are expected to sit on their computer and respond to inquiries. The time and mobility freedom they have will be different from that of a freelancer who can set their own schedule and only works thirty hours each week.

It's important to clearly define what you want because it's going to influence the rest of the job search process. Remote work can be a path to almost any lifestyle, but only if you specifically target the right remote positions and companies. Starting this process with a clear vision for your future will increase your odds of success. Your vision is your destination. It will guide all your actions and decisions, as well as keep you motivated during the inevitable ups and downs of the job search to come. Think of it this way: If you need a battery for your remote control, would you go to the store and buy the first battery you saw? Of course not. You'd first open the latch and look at what battery fits, and that would guide your decision of what to buy. That's the right approach for remote work too.

Change the Input: Reframe Your Mindset

*You are required to know what you want
before you can go and get it.*

In a noisy world full of confusion, a job search requires you to be laser-focused and clear about what you want. It is crucial you figure out quickly in this process which roles and types of companies you want to work for, based on what you want for your life. The more specific you get now, the better off you'll be in the future. If you pursue *every* job, you'll get *no* job.

The Benefits of Remote Work

As you begin thinking about lifestyle design, it's helpful to know what to expect from remote work. There are many advantages to working remotely, and understanding the benefits can guide your vision for your ideal life. Even if you've worked remotely before, it's good to get really clear on what benefits are most important to you in your next role as it will impact the types of companies you'll want to target.

FREEDOM OF LOCATION

For some, the dream is to work from home. The idea of getting out of bed, walking down the hall, and sitting down at their desk in their own house is appealing. It's a more comfortable environment, free from most of the restrictions, dress codes, and office politics of working on-site. Plus, their dog becomes a better coworker than anyone at the office.

For others, the dream is to throw off the shackles of all geographic restrictions, achieving true mobility that allows them to work anywhere in the world: a sidewalk café in Prague, a homestay villa in Bali, or a penthouse overlooking the rolling hills of Medellín.

While it's important to remember that many remote jobs have geographical restrictions of some kind, remote work is a huge step toward locational independence, which is important because it replaces *commute time* with *above-average free time*.

It presents you with more opportunities to experience the things you want, even if you don't gain significantly more time back. Choosing where you work and live, you automatically increase your *quality* of life outside of work. Living and having residency in Playa del Carmen, Mexico, for me, meant a mini-vacation every time I left my apartment.

Everyone's above-average free time looks different. For me, it means being in Mexico, where I can walk to the beach between Zoom calls. For you, it might be:

- Living in the Colorado mountains so you can snowboard or hike after work

- Roughing it on a farm in the middle of nowhere and raising chickens in your backyard

- RVing around the country, checking every national park off your bucket list

- Traveling all over the world, trying new foods, and meeting new people

- Practicing your hobbies, like taking breaks from deep work to learn a guitar chord

Whatever your above-average free time looks like, you have greater flexibility and freedom to make it happen as a remote worker.

TIME, TIME, AND MORE TIME

Being able to cut out the commute before and after work can free up a significant amount of time over the course of a week. If you commute half an hour each way, that's five hours a week. What could you do with an extra five hours each week? Go fishing at an aquarium until they kick you out? Drive around in a clown costume trying to scare people? Strategically place small garden gnomes in your neighbor's yard? Do you, I'm not judging.

Companies are also beginning to realize that when employees have more choice over their time, they're happier, healthier, and more productive during the times they are working. True remote-first culture cares more about output (work produced) than the input (hours put in). Instead of demanding you put in eight hours a day no matter what, what matters is you finish your work. If you can do that in six hours instead of eight, you get an extra two hours of your day back.

IMPROVED HEALTH

Remote work can also help you improve your health because, with more time, you can make your fitness and nutritional decisions with more intention. From personal experience, when I commuted to an office, I ate what was available, not what was healthy.

My first corporate job was in an IBM building about an hour outside of Boston, and we had a cafeteria on the lower level. It was easy to justify scarfing down my daily croissant, sausage, egg, and cheese with Sriracha because it was there. I mean, what were my options? I didn't have time to prepare meals, and I felt like I had to eat something. Being stuck in an office makes excuses easy to come by, and I never really stopped to question why I always felt like taking a nap by 10 a.m.

When you work remotely, healthy decisions become far more convenient. Suddenly, your environment allows you to trek a few steps down the hall to your kitchen for lunch. Now you've got the time, resources, and comfortability to mix up a leafy green salad and blend a protein shake rather than feeling forced to walk to the McDonalds a block away from the office.

The same idea applies to working out. During my office days, I was always tempted to skip the gym because I was exhausted. Working from home, it's much easier to squeeze in exercise during the day when it's best for my schedule.

You're also more likely to go to the doctor for regular checkups when you don't have to worry about taking paid time off. How many health problems go untreated because someone is reluctant to use their precious PTO?

BETTER RELATIONSHIPS

I don't have any kids that I'm aware of, but I imagine if you're raising a child, working from home enables you to be much more present in their life. I know some parents whose relationship with their kids was nonexistent because of their commute. They'd leave before their kids were up and come home after they were put in bed.

The alternative, being home with your kids throughout the day and available during breaks, changes your entire relationship, especially during the early years before they start school. You have more opportunities to create memories and can build a stronger, closer bond.

It's not only about kids. You have more time and attention to give to pets, a significant other, family, and friends. If a loved one needs you, you can be there for them. You can meet for lunch without worrying about rushing back to the office. You can send messages or call people when it's needed. You can even choose to move to be closer to your family. For many of my clients, their main motivation for finding remote work was to live closer to an aging parent, their significant other, or another family member either for a few months of the year or full-time.

People have this thought that working remotely means being lonely. But if you can work from anywhere, you can physically place yourself near the people you care about. In late 2018, I did an extended tour across the United States for three months—California, Oregon, Texas, Illinois, Hawaii, and Florida. I spent a week or two in each place. I was working, but in my free time, I got to hang out with friends I hadn't seen in years. I was also doing a YouTube video series at the time, *One Minute Weekly*, and I interviewed local entrepreneurs all across the country. I was traveling alone and working remotely, yet I was far from lonely. Location *independence* does not equal location *ambiguity*. You can make an intentional choice about where you want to be and who you want to be around. You can move not only your work location but your entire *life*.

Coworking and coliving spaces like Selina, Unsettled, and Outsite are becoming more common, which means it's easier than ever to plug yourself into a community. When I first started traveling, I took a four-month Remote Year trip across Europe and South Africa with fifty-plus strangers. It was one of the best experiences of my life.

Again, working remotely isn't perfect, but if done right, you can use it as a tool to prioritize new relationships, old relationships, or whichever ones you deem important.

COST SAVINGS

Populations are known to redistribute throughout history, but the pandemic combined with the rise of remote work led to a large exodus, especially for cities with populations exceeding one million, according to a Brookings analysis.

If you're not tied to a specific geographic location at work, you can choose to live somewhere with a lower cost of living. Rent prices in cities like New York or San Francisco are ridiculous. A 150-square-foot studio that feels like a jail cell runs you $2k+ a month. Housing inflation is likely only going to make that worse, but not before people move out in droves.

Not only can you save money by working remotely, but you can make money. Local governments are recognizing the opportunity to attract remote workers, and cities around the world are even offering to compensate people to move there!

There are many other cost savings associated with remote work, more than we can even discuss: childcare, parking fees, vehicle maintenance, property taxes, and so on.

The Challenges of Remote Work

Life is full of trade-offs. As we get deeper into how you want to design your life, it's important to be realistic about the challenges you'll face. The thing I love about *challenges* is that with a slight mental reframe, they can be seen as *opportunities*.

THE NEED FOR SELF-DISCIPLINE

Success as a remote worker requires a healthy amount of self-discipline because you won't have the same accountability structures as an on-site worker. Especially when first transitioning to remote work, many people struggle to stay self-motivated and productive. You'll be surrounded by distractions—kids, pets, your television staring at you from the corner in a tempting manner—and must learn not only how to prioritize work but how to prioritize the most important tasks.

If you don't have the will to build your discipline muscle, remote work will be miserable for you. Not only will you struggle to perform well in your job, but you won't be in a good position to take advantage of your freedom and the benefits of being remote. The good news is, self-discipline isn't something you're born with. It's a skill you can practice and get better at.

I recommend constantly self-auditing and building an environment that keeps you accountable. I journal, schedule virtual coworking sessions every day, have mastermind calls with peers, and create feedback loops that I otherwise wouldn't have on my own. Hell, I even make bets with accountability partners that I'll get a project done on a certain timeline, and if not, I'll have some sort of punishment. It's up to you to figure out what's going to push you, as different people are motivated by different things.

THE MYTH OF WORK-LIFE BALANCE

I never understood the idea of work-life balance, because it's not really possible. The idea of balance implies an ability to evenly distribute your time and energy among various aspects of your life. But life isn't distributed into clean and even buckets. Hell, you won't even be awake for a third of it, and outside of sleep, about a third of the waking hours left will be spent working. There is no such thing as *balance* in this reality.

The concept of work-life balance also seems to imply that humans are robots who can push an internal button on or off and cleanly compartmentalize what they're doing at work and what they do outside of it. But if you've ever had a bad night of sleep, fought with your significant other, or gotten sick, and tried to "tough it out" at work, you know that any of those things can heavily impact your work performance. Therefore, the thought that *work* is separate from *life* ignores the fundamental truth that to thrive as a remote worker means to care about yourself holistically—knowing that it all matters, and it's all connected.

Instead of trying the impossible feat of balance, why not try to integrate work into your ideal lifestyle? What if we accepted that your job makes a huge impact on the total quality of your life, and being able to do your job independent of location could improve your well-being? What if you enjoyed what you did, it was challenging and rewarding, and the company you worked for was aligned with your values? What if you enjoyed spending time with your coworkers because you actually believed in a common mission and were all empowered to live and work where you wanted?

This kind of integration is key to well-being, but it can be difficult to obtain. When you work remotely, especially from home, the line between work and life gets blurred. Instead of integrating, work starts to take over everything. Some people struggle to shut off their brain when they're "off the clock." If you work from home, you work where you also eat, sleep, and congregate with family. You may find it challenging to be fully present at dinner because you can still see your laptop on the counter, or you get an email ping on your phone. Having a designated workspace can help you prevent work from taking over. Turning off notifications outside work hours is also recommended.

Remote work is meant to improve your life, but if you don't find ways to integrate successfully, it may do the opposite.

LACK OF SOCIAL CONNECTION

The way you build relationships and interact with coworkers is different when you work remotely. Especially if you're an extrovert and you feed off others' energy, you might struggle with the lack of social connection during the day.

There are ways to mitigate this. Coworking spaces offer day passes or monthly subscriptions (some companies will even subsidize the cost for you). There are virtual coworking apps like Focusmate that pair you with people to work with all over the world. I've seen spacious cafés with bottomless coffee to entice customers to stay and work, and rooftop restaurants with five-course brunch menus and swimming pools littered with tables of digital nomads clicking away on their keyboards. These options can help you get more social connection while you're working. If that's not enough, you might consider a hybrid-remote position, where you spend at least a couple of days a week in an office setting if that gets you your fix.

On the other hand, remote work can pose challenges for introverts too. Some roles require a lot of calls in order to stay connected and collaborate over distance. Oftentimes people overcompensate with meetings (which could've just been an email), which can result in the dreaded "Zoom fatigue."

Changing your environment, intentionally building in social time, coworking, and more can help with these issues. The point is, it's still possible to build close relationships and strong social connections as a remote worker; it just takes more conscious effort. I also recommend focusing on the abundance of *choice* and intentionality you have for your social life outside of work when you work remotely, rather than focusing on the *lack* of social connection at work.

YOUR COMPETITIVE OPPORTUNITY

For any given remote position, there could be dozens, hundreds, or even thousands of interested applicants. And sometimes you're competing against not only people from your city or state, but from all over the country, or even the world.

Because you're competing against a larger candidate pool, you'll need to be even more strategic with how you apply and prove your value. Fortunately, you're smart. Do you know how I can tell? *You're reading this book!* Just by doing this, you're putting more intention into your search than 99% of job seekers. Unless this book sells really well, then maybe 98%.

Nonetheless, I want you to remember this: whenever you see one hundred applicants, you're not competing against all one hundred. Over half will be shit applications where the person didn't even read the listing and submitted their résumé as fast as possible. Most of them don't network with anyone at the company before applying, don't follow up on their application after submission, or do anything to look unique in the eyes of the employer.

This is why the challenge of competition actually becomes your opportunity. The more you do to stand out, the higher the barrier to entry is for others. When you take action that 99% of people don't do, you realize that your only true competition is yourself. That's the purpose of this book. I want you to be ready to take your remote job search to the next level.

Pro Tip: Be. Do. Have.

Oftentimes we think we need to *have* something to *do* something to *be* something (have, do, be). Thinking in that way is counterproductive. If you wait for an external factor to change in order to change your behavior, you won't get what you want. Many people don't recognize this, so they unknowingly get stuck in a loop.

Maybe you think you need to have some type of certification or experience before you can start even looking for a job. While having these things may help you, it's important to be aware of when your limiting beliefs are keeping you from moving forward and making progress.

Switching to "be, do, have" is a life-changing concept I learned from a mentor of mine, Louise Henry. Embodying the identity of the person you want to be is deeply impactful. There is a next-level version of you, let's call them *You 2.0*. Becoming You 2.0 isn't going to happen unless you decide to act like You 2.0 *before* you're ready. To discover You 2.0, ask yourself:

- Who do I need to be now to get the result that I want?

- How does that person act and make decisions?

- What would that person be doing on a daily basis?

> Always connect to You 2.0 with be, do, have, and make de-
> cisions as if you were the evolved version of yourself, not as the
> person you are today. You can even give them a name or an alter
> ego if you want. After a while of acting like the person you want
> to be, you'll just be them and more will be possible for you than
> you ever thought.

Visualize Your Future

To be able to get to the next chapter of your life, your mind needs to see that this future already exists. Don't skip this, as it becomes the foundation of your job search. (Note: Your responses to this exercise will change over time as you change, so it's useful to come back to this exercise every so often.)

Exercise: Designing Your Remote Life

Open the digital version of the following visualization exercise here: www.theremotejobcoach.com/book-resources.

First, do a "brain dump" of all your motivations for wanting to work remotely. Spend more time with family? No commute? Ability to travel? Once you have your list, identify the top three reasons.

Next, answer the big, important question: "What does my ideal life look like?" Your answer is going to impact how you search for a job, the types of companies you go after, and the roles you pursue. So take some time to actually imagine yourself there, living your future life. Go through your ideal day, hour by hour, and then your ideal week. How do you spend your time?

As an example, here's a breakdown of my idealistic, A+ day as it stands right now.

6:00–6:30 a.m.: Wake up. Drink some water, and do a quick round of breathwork or meditation with my BrainTap headset.

6:30–8:00 a.m.: Intensive cardiovascular movement, like boxing or HIIT classes.

8:00–8:30 a.m.: Short walk without any tech. Bonus points if the walk is on the beach in the sun.

8:30–9:30 a.m.: Sauna, cold plunge, and hot tub recovery circuit. Even better if the bros join (Shout out to Gabe, Al, Serge, Kumar, and Willis) for our "sauna talks."

9:30–10:30 a.m.: Intimate time with my partner. To my future wife reading this who I haven't met yet, I'm talking about you, of course.

10:30–11:00 a.m.: Work prep with a delicious smoothie (fruit, greens, matcha, and protein), morning journaling, and calendar review.

11:00–1:00 p.m.: Deep work on the most important thing of the day.

1:00–2:00 p.m.: Lunch break. Eat something light but nutrient-dense. Then take a quick walk, lay out in the sun for a bit, or jump in the pool to revitalize my energy levels.

3:00–4:00 p.m.: Creative time. Write, record a podcast, film a video, etc.

4:00–5:30 p.m.: Work calls, clear my inbox, make notes of unfinished tasks, and prep work for the next day.

5:30–7:00 p.m.: Pickup basketball at the local court.

7:00–8:30 p.m.: Nutritious and filling dinner. Even better when it's with a few good friends and invigorating conversation.

8:30–10:00 p.m.: Extroverted fun time. I prefer games, comedy shows, spiritual gatherings on the beach, and deep connection with others.

10:00–11:00 p.m.: Bedtime. Phone on airplane mode and open a good book until my eyes get heavy.

Now, is this how I live every day? Hell no! Have I ever lived this day? Like, once, I got pretty damn close to having this exact day. And that's exciting because I visualized it first before I knew that it existed! Belief is powerful, and this exercise gives me something to strive for. By visualizing and writing it out on paper, I'm also forced to consider the conditions necessary in my life to make it happen. It's the same for you.

For instance, you might notice that in my ideal remote workday I'm actually only working about four to five hours. To me, four focused and intentional hours are so much more powerful than eight lackadaisical ones (which is common in faux-performative office environments). This lets me know I either need to find a remote job with a company that's more focused on output than hours, or I need to work for myself. My ideal day also tells me a lot about the type of place I need to live— somewhere close to a gym, basketball court, beach, and spa. If you start with something as granular as the day you want to have, all of a sudden you can get clarity on everything you want.

Once you know what your ideal life looks like, visualize your ideal company. What's the work culture like? How big is it? What industry is it in? What product or service does it provide to the world? Then visualize your ideal role. Think about the level of autonomy, pay, job title, and so on.

Now bring it all together and prioritize what's most important to you in your job search, whether that's working in a particular industry or at a specific company, being able to travel, making a certain amount of money, or whatever.

See how this works when life goals, ambitions, and priorities come *first* before work? The opposite is being completely focused on work first, which has traditionally meant deciding where to move completely based on office location. Thinking about commute time and clocking in for a certain number of hours each day makes me want to vomit in my mouth. The point of remote work is that it offers more flexibility and choice. Whatever your ideal day and priorities are, remote work can be a tool to get you there.

From Vision to Reality

You're going to be spending a lot of time and effort on your job search, so why not put it toward the things you actually want? By taking the time to visualize your future and what you want from your work, you can better search for and find the right remote job for you. This is a far different approach than what most people do: scour job boards and click apply until your fingers go numb.

But knowing what you want and *getting* what you want are two different things. Defining your vision is a prerequisite, but it's not enough on its own. You need to *take targeted action* to make it a reality.

Every change in life starts with a first step, and that first step can be scary. Try thinking—and acting—as if the future you want has already happened, and time just needs to catch up. This could be more true than you realize. According to the multiverse theory, infinite parallel universes exist, so in some alternate universe, you're a king or queen who reigns supreme over a vast land of minions. If you've already done that in one universe, you can find a dope remote job in this one.

CHAPTER 3

ADJUST YOUR SETTINGS

Preparing for Remote Success

ONE WINTER MORNING IN 2013, I WOKE UP TO AN EMAIL THAT FELT like a message sent from God. I wiped the crust out of my eyes, read it slowly, then did a double-take. "Snowed in. Work from home today."

I rolled over in my bed, reset my alarm, and quietly rejoiced at the extra hour of sleep I just acquired. This was the first time in my corporate career I was allowed to work remotely, and honestly, I was just happy to have a buffer for my hangover to subside.

Since this first taste, I was addicted to remote work, and I was like a junkie who needed his fix.

The problem?

I was a shitty remote worker.

You don't just flip a switch and become an optimized, efficient remote employee just because your company tells you to stay home for the day. Nor does working remotely automatically fix all your problems. I realized, for me, it initially accentuated them. With too much flexibility and freedom, my natural reaction was to resist the difficult yet important things I was supposed to be doing.

It reminds me of when I was a preteen. There were times when I felt *slightly* sick. I definitely should've gone to school, but I was just sick enough to feign a deep cough and uncontrollable sniffling. Ultimately, I'd convince my mom I needed to stay home. I was fortunate that she was so nice, and I knew exactly what I could get away with. She'd call in to let the school know, and I'd rejoice knowing that ahead of me was a full day of trash TV without supervision, which meant my favorite show: Jerry Springer. If you don't know about the high-quality programming Jerry Springer was putting out in the '90s and early 2000s, you really missed out.

Staying home from school as a kid was akin to my "work from home" snow days at IBM. I remember being more concerned with appearing busy than actually doing anything. There were long days binging Netflix on the television with my laptop sitting next to me. Every now and then I'd move my mouse slightly to prevent my computer from falling asleep, all the while keeping my instant message icon set to "online" to avoid scrutiny.

I'm embarrassed to admit all this, but it's the truth. I know there are many people who, if they're being honest, have done the same. It didn't help that I was mentally depressed and didn't feel any connection to my purpose at the time. What I felt like doing was nothing, and that's what I did. People often do what they can get away with, especially if no one is keeping tabs on them.

Here's the thing: companies don't want shitty remote workers, and being a shitty remote worker can hold you back from the ideal life you visualized. If you put in the time, effort, and intentionality, remote work can be your greatest asset in life—but there's a learning curve to both remote work and the job search itself. You can offset that learning curve by making adjustments. Just like with a remote, you can improve the viewing experience by adjusting the picture resolution, sound setup, and language. Likewise, by changing your metaphorical settings—your mindset, your remote setup, and your work strategies—you can become a more appealing candidate and increase your odds of success in the job search.

Build the Right Mindset

How you think is how you act. I can predict how successful someone will be in their job search based solely on their mindset. Even if you're highly experienced or skilled, if your limiting beliefs are louder than the annoying construction outside of your hotel during a vacation, you're going to struggle. With the right mindset, even when you face obstacles, you'll overcome them and eventually land a remote job. The people who can reframe difficult experiences as learning lessons, handle rejection gracefully, and remain unattached to outcomes are the ones who enjoy the spoils of success. However, there are plenty of ways people get in their own way based on their thinking.

FAULTY ENTITLEMENT

Entitlement leads to laziness. Just because you need a remote job doesn't mean you deserve one. It's not my intention to sound condescending, but in my line of work, I meet a lot of people who feel entitled to an amazing, dream remote job with a company they love, yet they've done nothing to become the equal option for the company. None of these organizations owe you anything.

Look at yourself in the mirror, dig in, work hard, and show up for yourself. Be ready to prove that you're worth a shot. The harsh reality is, there are a lot of other people trying to do the same. While we'll go into exact strategies and tools for how to do this in later chapters, everything starts with your attitude and willingness to commit without a sense of entitlement.

IMPROPER EXPECTATIONS

Humans are piss-poor at setting expectations. We often either cata-strophize a situation and get obsessive about the worst-case scenario, or we're naively confident that nothing can go wrong. A job search will test your ability to set expectations for yourself. Your search is probably going to take longer than you think, and it might be harder than you hoped. The more you mentally prepare yourself for the long haul, the better you'll be able to face challenges and failures as they arise.

Simultaneously, if you go into this expecting to fail, that's what's going to happen. Success requires belief. The trick is to expect success while being unattached to the things you cannot control. All you can control is your effort, not the outcomes. If you focus on getting better and learning from the process, you'll be in much better shape. It's a tough line to walk, but expect the best and prepare for the worst.

EXPECTED DISCOURAGEMENT

Discouragement will happen. Things won't go according to plan. However, it's not discouragement you need to be concerned about. It's how you respond to discouragement that's important. I've met many people who give up in the face of adversity because they become so frustrated. By using this process, and committing to it, you'll be able to make a remote job happen—and it's your resolve that will be your greatest asset.

EXTREME OWNERSHIP

No one can want your success *for* you—not me, not a recruiter, not your family, not your friends, not a hiring manager. You have to want it for yourself, and you have to take full responsibility for your job search. Even when something goes wrong that doesn't feel like it's your fault, it's incumbent upon you to take ownership. Don't expect anyone to give you a job you haven't earned, and don't expect anyone to put in more effort than you.

HOW TO GAIN CONFIDENCE (4 C's)

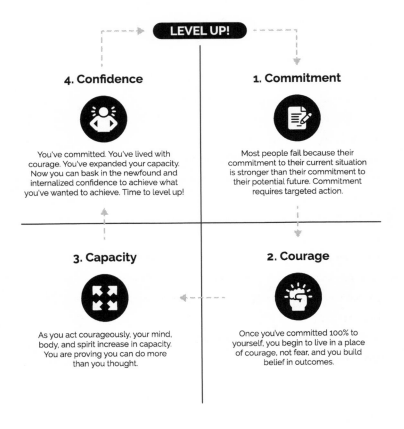

LEVEL UP!

4. Confidence

You've committed. You've lived with courage. You've expanded your capacity. Now you can bask in the newfound and internalized confidence to achieve what you've wanted to achieve. Time to level up!

1. Commitment

Most people fail because their commitment to their current situation is stronger than their commitment to their potential future. Commitment requires targeted action.

3. Capacity

As you act courageously, your mind, body, and spirit increase in capacity. You are proving you can do more than you thought.

2. Courage

Once you've committed 100% to yourself, you begin to live in a place of courage, not fear, and you build belief in outcomes.

A key aspect of your mindset is confidence, even in the face of uncertainty. If you're not feeling confident at this point, that's normal. Often, we look at confident people and assume they're naturally confident, as if it were a genetic trait they were born with. However, that's not the case.

I had a coach who once taught me a valuable lesson on how to gain confidence that forever changed the way I think about it. Since cultivating confidence is so important to achieving your goals, I'm sharing this with you to help you gain more confidence not only in your job search, but in all the things you want to achieve in life.

- **Step #1: Commitment**—Most people who fail do so because their commitment to their current situation is stronger than their commitment to their potential future. You don't have to know exactly *how* you're going to achieve your vision yet. You just have to decide you're going to make it happen. By reading this book, you're already demonstrating commitment. Commitment is strongest when it requires financial and time investments.

- **Step #2: Courage**—Once you are 100% committed to the job search, you'll begin to feel more courageous. With newfound determination, your belief in yourself will compound, and you'll naturally overcome previous fears you had.

- **Step #3: Capacity**—As you begin to act with courage, your mind, body, and spirit will gradually increase in capacity, and you will discover you can accomplish more than you initially thought.

- **Step #4: Confidence**—As you accomplish more, your confidence in your ability to take action and achieve your goal will grow. Seeing is believing! You'll internalize this confidence, and these simple steps will become your superpower for leveling up in life.

Commitment is the key. It's the catalyst that sets off a domino effect to confidence. Think about anything difficult you've achieved in your life. Even if you didn't realize it at the time, every single one of your accomplishments required a commitment on your part. Once you commit, the universe will conspire with you as everything starts to fall in place.

Take a deep breath, a really deep breath. Are you 100% committed to this remote job search and ready to make it happen for yourself? Being intentional about making this commitment is one of the most crucial things you can do. Recognize that if you choose not to make this commitment, you are still committing to something: your current reality.

Construct the Right Remote Environment

After cultivating your mindset and making a mental commitment, the next way to prepare for success is by assembling your environment to work for you.

It's worth making an investment in your remote setup so you have the tools and equipment to work comfortably. In my early days of remote work, I set up shop at the kitchen table in an old wooden dining chair, or from the comfort of my bed, lying back with my computer on my lap. Each day I'd pick my poison: run the risk of ass splinters and back pain from sitting on a pile of sticks with armrests, or falling asleep because the combo of a painfully boring all-hands call and my memory foam mattress produced a predictable outcome. Let's just say the quality of my work was affected by my environment.

Even if you're not working remotely yet, it's still important to create a supportive environment beforehand, because it impacts the impression you make and the confidence you have in yourself. For example, if you were to finally land a video interview with your favorite remote company, how you come across during the call will be the main reference point they have of what it's like to work with you. What sort of impression will it make if the person on the other end of the line has a hard time hearing or seeing you? If your connection cuts out, or you seem distracted by your surroundings? If you're sitting in a messy room, or somewhere with a lot of background noise?

A hiring manager or recruiter might think, "Do I want this person representing our company? What sort of image will they convey? Do they even take their work seriously?"

In contrast, a great remote setup will make you look like you're ready and qualified to be a remote worker—even if you don't have a lot of remote work experience!

Whether you're applying for a remote position, having virtual conversations with employees at a remote company, or already working remotely, the right environment will set you up for success.

My purpose with this section is not to goad you into buying a bunch of stuff you can't afford in order to create an unnecessarily lavish workspace. Rather, I want you to be aware of the deficiencies created by a lackluster workspace because the environment you create impacts everything. I'm a big proponent of investing in quality when you're purchasing items you're going to use daily so they'll last. In this section, we'll cover a few key aspects of your remote setup that will make the biggest difference.

Resource: Remote Essentials

For a list of all my remote essentials, visit www.theremotejobcoach. com/remote-essentials.

CRISP AUDIO

As you can imagine, how well people can hear you matters tremendously when you're working remotely. Despite this, many people rely on their computer microphone to get the job done. Depending on the acoustics in the room, background noise, or if you're typing, it can be impossible to hear you.

According to Blue, the manufacturer who makes the mic I use (Blue Snowball USB mic):

In order to discreetly fit inside your computer, built-in laptop microphones are extremely small, which limits their ability to accurately capture sound. Most laptop mics also boost harsh midrange frequencies to help vocals "cut through" other sounds, which can be difficult to listen to for extended periods of time. Because of this, they pick up every little bit of background noise, like barking dogs, crying babies, and your neighbor's lawn mower.

So unless you want loud babies and puppies to be the star of your Zoom calls, consider the kind of audio experience you're creating for the people on the other end of the line. If you invest in a solution to come in loud and clear, they'll notice the difference, even if you don't.

You can buy a very affordable, simple USB microphone, or even wired headphones with an attached mic. There are two considerations as part of this process. One is your audio input, one is your output. Depending on the kind of mic you get, you may want to invest in headphones as well to serve as your audio output—otherwise, the audio coming out of your computer will be picked up by your mic and create an annoying echo.

Digital Nomad Pro Tip: To save space and travel efficiently, find quality headphones with an attached mic. Wired Apple headphones work well from my experience. I always travel with two pairs because I inevitably step on or lose them at some point.

CLEAR VIDEO

Your audio quality is substantially more important than your video quality, but a good picture quality is still valuable, especially because video calls are so prevalent.

Remember the subconscious messages you send to recruiters, hiring managers, and potential coworkers. Think about the impression it makes when someone shows up to a video call with a blurry, grainy video that looks like it's being shot from a potato.

It reminds me of this quote by T. Harv Eker, "How you do anything is how you do everything." The little details matter! Whether right or wrong, if someone's video is so bad that it's distracting, it's not a stretch to think that person doesn't have experience working remotely or isn't equipped properly to succeed.

I recommend using a 1080p webcam if you can afford the investment. However, if you're forced to choose between good audio equipment and good video equipment, prioritize audio every time! As long as the webcam on your computer is decent enough, you can take a pass for now, but think carefully about how you want to look when you show up on a call. With good video quality, you'll send the message you're serious about remote work and invested in being productive.

Digital Nomad Pro Tip: Most external webcams are small and can be easily stored in a backpack. I bring mine in a small case everywhere I go. But if you're going to be traveling a lot and have a decent enough webcam on your computer, you may opt to save space.

Pro Tip: Think About Lighting

As any good photographer knows, lighting is key. To look your best on camera, place a light or position yourself with a light right behind your computer or camera, so people can see your face. You can purchase a ring light for cheap, but even a desk lamp or sitting in the right spot with overhead light or natural light from a window makes a big difference. Avoid sitting in the dark and looking like a movie villain every time you're on a video call.

DEDICATED SPACE

Think about how you can create a dedicated workspace free from distractions and equipped with the right tools. If possible, designate a room or part of your house, apartment, or living space that is away from entertainment, other people, and interruptions.

Even if you can't eliminate or prevent all distractions (e.g., parents during the pandemic who had children in virtual school), do what you can to segment a place that feels like your own personal workspace. Even a corner of a room will work. The point is to try to set boundaries, as this helps your brain associate a specific location with productivity.

Digital Nomad Pro Tip: Look up accommodations well in advance before you stay somewhere to give yourself time to find places that are either furnished with a desk or give you access to some type of workspace. When I travel, I filter the amenities on Airbnb, with "dedicated workspace" as one of my minimum requirements.

ERGONOMIC DESK AND CHAIR

Whatever you spend the most time using, consider investing a proportionate amount to find something of high quality. That's to say, if you're going to be sitting in one chair every day, you don't want to sit on a chair made of pointed branches like I used to. Finding something comfortable and ergonomic is worth it, and your back and ass will thank you.

If you plan to work in the same space each day, it's also worth investing in a nice desk. Think about the things you commonly keep in your workspace, such as notebooks, coffee cups, pet rocks, water bottles, and find a desk big enough to fit it all. Maybe a standing desk works better for you, in which case you can even get a converter. Whatever the case, you can usually find a good deal on a new desk and chair on Amazon or used ones on Craigslist, OfferUp, Facebook Marketplace, or even your local thrift and consignment shops.

Digital Nomad Pro Tip: I highly recommend the BetterBack support for all types of remote workers. It's the best back support I've found on the market. It helps improve your posture, and for those on the go, it folds up into an easy travel pouch. I bring it everywhere I go as it can make even the worst chairs tolerable.

RELIABLE CONNECTIVITY

Internet access of some kind is an absolute requirement for remote work, and a connection speed of 10 Mbps is the bare minimum. Don't rely on WiFi if you don't have to. Get an ethernet cord and connect directly to your router. This helps to improve the quality of your internet connection, and you'll notice the difference. In my own experience, the speed of my internet increased by 20 Mbps when I first switched from WiFi to an ethernet cord.

Digital Nomad Pro Tip: WiFi numbers can be misleading. When you're traveling, do as much as you can to confirm beforehand not only the Mbps upload and download speed, but how reliable the bandwidth and latency are. I've been in places that seemed to have good WiFi only to find out the connection fluctuates more than the price of Bitcoin. If you're ever doing tours for an upcoming stay, always, always, always ask to test the internet. There are plenty of speed test apps you can use.

Create Great Systems and Workflows

As *Atomic Habits* author James Clear has said, "You do not rise to the level of your goals. You fall to the level of your systems." While the tools you choose are important to a degree, the systems and workflows you put in place matter even more because they become the guardrails for your success.

The way you work, interact with data, and execute on a daily basis matters because the hours you have available are limited. By creating the foundation for your productivity and making adjustments to iterate and improve, you can compound the impact on your success.

A lot of people get wrapped up in selecting the right tech—like spending hours researching the perfect time-tracking app—and don't dedicate enough thought to why it's important for them to even bother tracking their time in the first place. Like a rattle to an impressionable baby, there will always be shiny new apps to distract and consume your attention. But with the right underlying systems and workflows, you can adapt to any potential tool out there.

If you already work remotely, the skills and strategies in this section will help you become more productive. If you aren't working remotely yet, all these things still apply to you. Why? The more you understand what's important in remote work, and start acting like a remote worker, the better chance you have of getting hired.

And guess what: you *are* a remote worker. Your remote job is finding a remote job.

Exercises: Systems and Workflows

Visit www.theremotejobcoach.com/book-resources for a variety of exercises that can help you improve your systems and workflows.

JOURNAL CONSISTENTLY

Journaling is one of the best tools for reflection and improvement, not only in your job search, but in your life. It's a way to track your progress and build self-awareness, as well as develop an understanding of what brings you happiness and fulfillment.

I've been journaling since 2015. I use *The Five Minute Journal* by Intelligent Change, which has prompts for the morning and evening.

When I wake up I write about my gratitude for the day, tasks I'd like to complete, and affirmations. Just before I go to sleep, I summarize what went well and what could have made the day even better. Having a guided journal that only takes a few minutes is a game changer for me because it makes the process quick and easy to be consistent.

At the end of the week on Sunday, I'll revisit each day and copy what I wrote into a Google Doc. That way, I've virtualized all of my entries and can easily sort and see dates across multiple journals. By revisiting them I'm also reminding myself of the wins that happened, internalizing the lessons I learned, and building momentum.

CONDUCT TIME AUDITS

As Ramit Sethi, an entrepreneur and author of *I Will Teach You to Be Rich,* said, "Show me someone's calendar and spending, and I'll show you what their priorities are." I agree. How you spend your time (and money) reveals what actually matters to you. Since humans are creatures of habit, a lot of the time we spend is determined by subconscious behaviors. The result? We often end up acting on autopilot.

You already have routines, whether you realize it or not. When you wake up each morning, what do you do? Get on your phone and check Twitter? Make a cup of coffee? Jump in the shower? How about when you sit down at your desk each day? Do you check your email? Dive into deep work?

We naturally form habits, repeating the same behavior again and again. This autopilot isn't always a bad thing. Routines provide structure, and they make it easier to be productive because you don't spend energy figuring out what you're going to do. You just do it. When we're not intentional about our routines, though, we're more likely to develop habits that work against our progress.

The first step to addressing a problem is awareness, so I encourage you to conduct regular time audits—an examination of how you're spending your days—to get an idea of what's actually important to you, not what you lie to yourself about and just say is important.

I'll go first. This book took me over two years to write, and there was a period of time for multiple months where I spent zero hours per week on writing. Yet when talking to people, I would mention writing this book and how important it was to me. I wasn't intentionally lying, because I *felt* like the book was important to me, but the reality of how I spent my time told a different story. I see this a lot with job seekers who say they want to change their life yet spend zero time on the activities that would move the needle on their job search.

Now, let's get back to you.

In order to do an audit, you need to lay it all out on the table. The first step is to do a brain dump of all your current habits and routines. These are things you do on a daily, weekly, or monthly basis. Don't discriminate, write everything you can think of. The goal is to find the missing gaps between your current life and the visualization of your ideal, remote life. Be as honest as possible in your assessment of yourself. Here are a few ways you can brainstorm:

- Start with what comes top of mind—the things you do all the time. Simply pay attention.

- Open up your bank statements and see what you spend your money on.

- If you keep a journal, check out your past entries.

- Look at the events in your calendar.

- Check your screen usage statistics on your phone.

- Scroll through your photos and social media posts to jog your memory.

The initial time audit is just to create a large list of things you do consistently without judgment. Now that we have this list, it's time to be a bit more judgmental.

ESTABLISH THOUGHTFUL ROUTINES WITH TACK

Once you know how you spend your time, you can start consciously creating the routines you want, deciding what activities you want to trim, what to add, what to cut, and what to keep.

- Trim—These serve you when done less, so you'd like to trim the frequency or duration.

- Add—These are habits you want to add to your routine.

- Cut—These don't serve you, and you want to cut them completely.

- Keep—These help you move toward your ideal life and goals.

Once I realized I wasn't treating my book like a priority, I decided to add a morning routine of writing. As I'm writing this section right now, it's 8:00 a.m. and I've been writing since 5:30 a.m. I'll go for another half hour or so, and then get back to it again tomorrow morning. Now when I tell someone how important this book is to me, deep down I know it's true because I'm spending two to three hours every morning before the sun is up to get this thing done.

If finding a remote job is truly one of your biggest priorities, then strive to spend a healthy chunk of your day on the activities that contribute to your potential success. That includes more than applying online. It also means assembling routines to build relationships with relevant companies, establishing your personal brand, practicing and developing the skills to be an effective remote worker, and so on (we'll go over these in the coming chapters). Creating space in your day might require sacrifices like cutting or trimming Netflix time, but once you make these decisions, your time spent will reflect your actual priorities.

MAKE YOUR CALENDAR YOUR BEST FRIEND

Now that you've got your habits sorted on paper, it's time to create a system to stay accountable to them. Your calendar is the best way to do this. For me, if something isn't on the calendar, it doesn't exist. I schedule everything from my morning routine, to personal meetings, to recurring deep work blocks, to comedy shows I'm going to with friends. I've even got my lunch breaks in there as if I would completely forget to eat if they weren't (I have).

Your calendar, if used strategically, can become your sole source of truth of what's happening in your life, like a virtual Morpheus that guides you on your quest for productivity. If you don't like Matrix references, using an effective calendar is like outsourcing your brain without needing to be the main character of a dystopian *Black Mirror* episode. The less you have to think or make decisions about what you're going to do during a day, the easier it is to just execute the most important thing. Especially in the beginning of establishing new habits, it's too easy to forget what the hell you were going to do and when the hell you were going to do it.

When I start working with clients, one of the first things we do is create their new schedule by starting with their "non-negotiables." Those might be family time, required work tasks, exercise, or anything else that needs to get done each week no matter what. From there, we find an hour or two a day that they're going to commit to their job search and put a time block in their calendar. When we schedule routines, they're much more likely to happen.

ACCESS FLOW WITH DEEP WORK

Deep work—an elongated period of time where you focus on one task—is huge for productivity. We're conditioned to think that doing multiple things at once is productive. However, multitasking simply splits your focus between multiple tasks, leaving lots of unused brain juice on the table, and no task gets your full energy.

Instead of flying by the seat of your pants all day, reactively responding to emails and Slack messages like a soldier fielding enemy fire from the trenches, take a proactive stance on your workday by accessing a flow state with deep work:

1. Block out deep work time on your schedule.

2. Set a clear intention and an effort-based outcome. Focus on only what you can control and set some tangible success criteria for the session. For example, if you're networking with people at your target company, the success would be the number of people you reach out to, not the number that responds (because you can't control that).

3. When the time starts, put your phone on airplane mode, turn off email notifications, and close any apps or unnecessary browser tabs not related to the task at hand to prevent distractions.

4. I usually set a timer for fifty minutes. If you're new to deep work, start with shorter sessions of twenty-five minutes each. Over time, as you train your brain, increase the length or number of sessions.

5. Work uninterrupted and focused!

6. After you finish your allotted deep work time, evaluate how you did. Figure out where you got distracted or hung up and

make adjustments. If you find you've overestimated (or under-estimated) how much you can get done in your chosen time period, recalibrate for next time.

7. Take a five- or ten-minute break. Get some tea or water. Go to the bathroom. Walk around a little. Giving your mind a short rest will help you avoid burnout.

8. Repeat.

Try to do at least one or two hours of deep, uninterrupted work a day, five days a week. You'll be amazed at how much more you can get done. It can also be extremely helpful to find a partner or community to cowork with for your deep work sessions.

Sometimes I facilitate deep work sessions with my clients. We jump into a virtual room, everyone says what they are going to do, and the social accountability pushes people to do their best. I've had clients say they've done more in one facilitated deep work session to progress on their job search than entire weeks of job seeking while distracted.

Outside of hosting coworking myself, I love to use tools like Focusmate, an online app that pairs you with other professionals around the world who are committed to being accountable for finishing their most important work. Huge props to my buddy Taylor for creating such an awesome resource for remote workers.

Besides helping you supercharge your job search, true remote work is based on output, which makes deep work even more crucial for remote workers. Fortunately, your ability to do deep work is like a muscle—the more you exercise it, the better you'll get at it, and the more productive you'll be.

BATCH YOUR TASKS

Every time you switch from one type of task to another, you create an interruption. This can cause a loss of focus and productivity. By batching your work and focusing on a singular type of task during a block of time, you can be more productive.

Using the job search as an example, let's say you have an hour on a Monday morning to commit. You might start by looking at job boards and end up finding a listing you like. From there, you open a tab with the company's website and start clicking on different links. You skim their "About" page, then notice they have a YouTube channel. You start watching one of their videos about a recent acquisition announcement, and one of the videos in the "suggested" section looks really interesting: "How to Start an Affiliate Marketing Business." You click on that. Thirty minutes later, after becoming an expert affiliate marketer, you're startled by your timer going off. Your job search hour is up, and somehow without realizing it, you're five minutes into a video called "How to Introduce a Dog to a Cat." What the hell just happened? Because there was no strategy behind the work session, there were too many types of tasks, and it went off the rails.

If you've ever been on the internet, you know these death spirals are more common than video calls that should've been emails. To avoid falling into the wormhole, focus on only one type of task at a time. While we'll get more into exact job search strategies later in the book, let me give you an example of how it can be done differently.

On Monday, you add new target companies to your list. You don't want to go down the wormhole, so you don't do any research yet; you simply set an alert with the company and save their link without being too critical. Then on Tuesday, you do a deeper dive on three of the companies you saved, determining what jobs they have available and your alignment to their values. On Wednesday, you go through LinkedIn and find potential employees to network with. You don't message them in the moment; you simply save their profiles, so you don't go down those wormholes again. Then on Thursday you go back and send messages to at least one or two employees at each of the companies. And so on and so forth.

If you were to try to save companies, do extensive research, find employees, and send messages all in one hour, it would be overwhelming. Even if you managed to avoid distracting wormholes, constantly switching the type of job search task would reduce the quality of each one significantly. By splitting them up into one-hour segments each, it becomes much easier to set an intention and execute.

If I hammer anything home into your brain with this book, let it be an appreciation of quality over quantity. Deep over shallow. Long-term over short-term.

STACK YOUR WINS

I sat there in a Florida convention center surrounded by ten thousand strangers. It was late 2017, and after a rough breakup and an existential quarter-life crisis, I bought a ticket to a Tony Robbins seminar called Unleash the Power Within. Among many life-changing takeaways, I remember him saying, "Where focus goes, energy flows." What we choose to fixate on the most in our lives is what we get more of. If you focus on how you're winning, you'll find more wins. If you focus on losing, you'll find more losses.

The best part about the universe is that it doesn't distinguish between a *small* win and a *big* win. It only distinguishes between energy. Nothing has given me more positive momentum in my life than my constant focus on recognizing good things that are happening to me. The best way to focus on wins is to write them down—yet another reason to start a journaling practice.

Recognizing your wins will set you up for continued success in the future, and if you're ever struggling, you can go back in time to remember the progress you've already made to encourage you to keep going.

Manage Your Energy in the Job Search

As humans, we often vastly underestimate how much energy and focus a given task will require. Have you ever reflected on a long eight- to ten-hour day and thought, "What the hell did I actually accomplish?"

This can easily become a major source of frustration if you're working while searching for a job outside of work hours. Learning some tactics to manage your energy will help prevent burnout.

PRIORITIZE THE MOST IMPORTANT THING

If you want to make progress in your job search, it must be a priority in the way you act. You might need to continue working your current job for financial reasons, but you've already determined it's not the future you want; your new job is.

To make the most progress toward your desired future, spend at least an hour of your most productive time of the day on your job search if possible. Maybe that's first thing in the morning or later in the evening—whenever your mind is at its sharpest.

I've had clients wake up an hour earlier every morning before their kids are up to make sure they can work undistracted before making breakfast and then commuting to an office. Some have taken coaching calls with me from their car in the parking lot while on lunch break. One of my clients even listened to my course videos while working on a car assembly line at the Tesla factory (you'll learn more about him later). There will always be excuses if you want to make them, but the way you act in spite of your circumstances speaks the loudest.

Just know that not everything is urgent, and most job seekers are misallocating their time by spending most of it on actions that are unlikely to move the ball forward. If LinkedIn's "Easy Apply" button to you is like a shiny toy to a kid with ADHD, then we need to change things!

THE POWER OF TINY GAINS

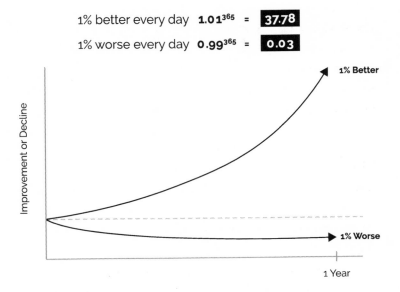

1% better every day 1.01^{365} = **37.78**

1% worse every day 0.99^{365} = **0.03**

1% Better

Improvement or Decline

1% Worse

1 Year

The simple, small decisions and actions we take every day have a compounding effect that vastly impacts our future. The 1% rule (popularized by author James Clear) demonstrates this power. If you get just 1% better each day, it may not seem like a lot. But when you run the numbers, by the end of the year, you will be *thirty-seven times* better.

It's more fruitful to put in an hour or two of strong, focused job searching every day than to do six or seven hours at a time once a week. Consistency brings opportunity and keeps your mind fresh on the relevant information and progress you're making.

The tools, techniques, and strategies I share throughout this book are intended to provide a long-term solution, not a short-term fix. That means they're not one-and-done activities. Any job change is a process, and my goal is to help set you up for success for the rest of your life. Even after you find a job, don't stop using these techniques. If you don't want to be in a constant position of starting from zero, be consistent over time and you'll always be able to pivot.

BUILD A SUPPORT SYSTEM

Everyone needs a support system, and during a job search, it can be vital to your ability to combat discouragement. Most job seekers don't even know what they're doing wrong, and you can't expect true, actionable feedback from recruiters and hiring managers. They just don't have the time. Surround yourself with other people who are going through the same thing and find an expert to guide you. This opens up positive feedback loops that you simply can't access on your own.

In my coaching masterminds and group calls focused on remote job searching, sometimes the biggest strides a client makes are when someone else with a similar issue receives coaching on the subject. When we are too close to our own problems, we have blind spots. Watching someone else deal with a relatable problem helps us see a path to solving our own.

It's particularly helpful to hang out with other people who already work remotely because they can share stories, tips, motivation, and maybe even leads to jobs! There are tons of communities online that can help support you. Late in the book I'll name some specific ones that have helped me outside of my own.

QUIT IF YOU CAN

If you're currently working, especially in a self-destructive and toxic environment, consider quitting if it's financially feasible. Obviously, if you can dedicate all your time and energy to your job search, instead of splitting it with your current role, you'll be able to make more progress, more quickly.

If you do decide to quit or are unemployed, treat your job search like a full-time job. Devoting forty-plus hours a week and your full energy and attention with the right strategy will drastically improve your chances of success.

Begin the Job Search!

Now that we've laid the right foundation, we can get started on the job search! Whether you've never worked remotely before or you're a remote expert looking for your next challenge, let's get you closer to your ideal job and life based on your skills and experience.

CHAPTER 4

REWIND

Use Your Past Skills and Experience to Your Advantage

KEVIN WAS A PIT BROKER IN THE CHICAGO MERCANTILE EXCHANGE. Being in the financial sector, his career was very "traditional," but as he started to reevaluate some of his goals in life, he realized he wanted something different.

He wanted more freedom. He wanted to travel and experience the world. He wanted a remote job, but it felt like an unattainable dream. He had never worked remotely before and even went so far as to call himself the "least likely candidate who could do remote work" because his experience and skillset didn't seem transferable to the remote world. "I never thought I would ever do anything else," he told me. His trader friends thought the same thing. When he told them he was leaving the industry, they said, "Yeah, right. You'll be back."

He'd been intrigued by coding before and decided to invest in an online boot camp to accelerate his skills and chances of success. While it was daunting to start a completely new career in his thirties, he picked up things quickly. He bolstered his technical abilities by learning to code, but despite his new skill, he was having trouble articulating his past experiences and understanding how they'd be relevant to what he was doing now.

When Kevin finished the boot camp, he applied to be a tutor for the students. It became both a great stepping stone to get more relevant experience and a way to fortify his skills by teaching. We worked together to craft his LinkedIn and résumé to highlight transferable skills he learned from the financial sector and align them to his new industry. He began to see the possibilities, and these options gave him a supreme bout of confidence.

He then landed his first freelance project: helping one of his friends who owned a financial company build a trading tool. He was the perfect person for the job because he had not only the coding skills but also a financial background and understanding of the industry. All those skills Kevin thought weren't transferable were exactly what helped him stand out in this niche.

What I also love about Kevin's story is that he found a new passion for teaching. He landed a position as a teaching assistant at a university, something he was able to do while simultaneously traveling the world. Over the time span that Kevin and I worked together, he lived in Barbados via their digital nomad visa, Dubai, and also spent time in the US with his family when his nephew was born. He leveraged his credibility in the financial industry to niche down and use his applicable skills in the best way possible. Not only that, but he took practical stepping stones, whether doing the boot camp to learn a new skill, tutoring to get more experience, or becoming a teacher's assistant to earn a paycheck.

Kevin's life looks completely different from his days on the trading room floor. Instead of being built around choices and options in the stock market, it's now built around choices and options of what's important to him (see what I did there?). Despite his friends' predictions, he hasn't gone back to the trading floor, and he doesn't plan to.

The job search can be intimidating, and a remote position may feel impossible. But you *can* make the transition, just like Kevin. Whether you know it or not, if you hit rewind, you can find experiences and skills from your past that can be transferred to a remote job, and you can develop new skills if necessary. If you're already working remotely and know what type of role you're best fit for, you'll be able to skip or skim several sections in this chapter, but unless you already have your dream remote job (in which case, why are you reading this book?!), you can benefit from understanding how to best leverage your skills and experience.

Change the Input: Reframe Your Mindset

No one's path is linear.

I've worked with people who want it all: a remote lifestyle, a job they're passionate about, and a nice salary. It's possible to achieve all those things, but reaching your vision isn't linear for anyone these days, it's a process that goes in all sorts of directions. Instead of waiting around for the perfect position (and getting frustrated when it doesn't exist), take one step at a time to move toward more freedom. As you take on new roles and get more experience working remotely, you're going to learn more about what you do and don't want, while simultaneously making yourself more competitive as a candidate. Especially if you've never worked remotely before, it can be helpful to get any *relevant* remote work experience. It'll give you a good jumping-off point for your next step. As long as you keep moving closer to your vision, twists and turns in your path are to be expected. Fall in love with that part—the process—and life becomes a lot more enjoyable.

Build a Path of Stepping Stones

The right remote job matches your skills and the vision of your ideal lifestyle. The problem is, like Kevin, there might be a gap between your current skills and your vision. Big changes sometimes require a path of stepping stones. Especially if you haven't worked remotely before, or you are entering an entirely new industry or skill area, be realistic about the "low-hanging fruit." This is the first goal I recommend to clients. I try to help them discover what in their specific case is the easiest pathway to the remote life they desire and guide them in taking steps to move closer to their vision from there.

When changing jobs, there are a number of variables, or levers, at play that will impact the difficulty of the transition:

- Remote vs. office
- Job role
- Industry
- Company size
- Work culture

The more levers you pull at once, the more difficult the transition will be, meaning that both getting the job and succeeding in the job will be more challenging. Trying to move to a new role, a new industry, a different-size company, and a different work culture all at once is exponentially more difficult than changing just one of those variables. I'm not saying that biting off a big piece to chew is impossible, but it increases your chances of choking. Be thoughtful about how many variables you're changing at once, especially if you're transitioning to remote work for the first time.

The job you get now doesn't have to be the job you'll have forever. If it gets you closer to your vision, it's still valuable.

Translatable Soft Skills

Skills are the currency you use in the remote job marketplace to obtain employment and opportunities. It's crucial you're able to articulate your various skills with proof of how they've helped you succeed at prior organizations and why they're relevant to the new company you're interested in working for.

When you think of remote skills, your mind might immediately jump to marketable hard skills like programming or graphic design, but the soft skills of remote work are arguably more important. Soft skills are the ancillary abilities we pick up along the way that help us work more effectively, especially in teams. Their importance in remote work is heightened since they require additional ability to translate them to fully virtual environments.

You could be known as the Mozart of coding, but if you're a terrible communicator who lacks emotional intelligence and empathy, you're like a delicious chicken parmesan that was dropped into a mud puddle. Yes, you need to be competent, but more and more companies are hiring for attitude and aptitude. No one wants to work with a complete asshat who sucks the energy out of every Zoom room.

Developing key soft skills will help you level up as a remote worker.

- **Digital proficiency**—As a remote worker, digital proficiency is a prerequisite. According to CMSWire, digital proficiency is "the measure of capacity to use digital technologies to one's benefit." It is less about your skill with any single tool and more about your ability to adapt and learn to navigate new tools within a reasonable amount of time.

- **Emotional intelligence**—According to Indeed, emotional intelligence is the ability to recognize, understand, and manage your own emotions as well as being able to understand and influence the emotions of others. In work environments emotional intelligence is tested constantly, especially in teams where employees are distributed throughout the world from various cultural and national backgrounds.

- **Self-motivation and autonomy**—Remote work comes with freedom, which can be a curse as well as a blessing. Ask honestly: Are you able to get shit done without someone telling you exactly what to do? Can you find answers with limited instructions? When you wake up in the morning with your office just steps away, can you get yourself to work?

- **Strong written communication**—The better communicator you are, the more opportunities you'll have not only in remote work but in life. This is why writing is the most valuable skill you can cultivate. In a remote position, you won't be able to stroll to your boss's desk to ask a question or pop your head over the cubicle wall to explain something to your coworker. It's critical you develop strong written communication skills.

- **Teamwork and collaboration**—In a remote environment, teamwork and collaboration don't happen as naturally as they do in a physical workplace. Being able to excel at working with others at distance is a must have.

- **Organization**—Without a single centralized location for all employees, companies need to know you can keep yourself organized. Being organized includes prioritization of the most important tasks, keeping clean records, documenting processes, and preventing responsibilities from slipping through the cracks.

- **Time and energy management**—Having time to do something doesn't always mean having the energy to do it. Working remotely, the two components are interconnected. The better you're able to divide your days to be productive based on your energy levels, the more successful you'll be.

- **Problem-solving**—Remote work comes with unique challenges. Maybe you're supposed to lead a presentation for a major customer, but it's hurricane season and your power gets knocked out for a week (this happened to me in Mexico). Or perhaps a coworker is offline because he's in the delivery room with his wife who's having their baby, and he has all the files you need to meet a deadline. Your ability to adapt and problem-solve will help you meet and overcome the challenges that come with remote work.

These are by no means the only soft skills helpful in remote work, but they're a good foundation from which to start.

Resources: Digital Proficiency

To get an understanding of where your digital proficiency currently stands, visit www.theremotejobcoach.com/book-resources for additional resources.

Marketable Hard Skills

Hard skills are the things we've typically done training for, had education in, or have experience doing. While more jobs are shifting to remote, not all hard skills are easily transferable. Based on research as well as my experiences and my client's experiences, certain hard skills pop up again and again. Underneath each skill area, I've included three example positions for you to consider. Note that these examples are not the only options, but they provide a good reference point for what's in demand as of the writing of this book:

- Accounting and Finance
  - Accountant, billing coordinator, financial analyst

- Education
  - Curriculum developer, language teacher, tutor

- HR and Legal
  - Human resources generalist, legal counsel, recruiter

- Marketing, Media, and Design
  - Digital marketer, graphic designer, social media manager

- Project and Program Management
  - Product manager, program manager, project manager

- Sales and Business Development
  - Account manager, customer success representative, sales representative

- Technology
  - Cyber security analyst, machine learning engineer, web developer

This list is by no means exhaustive, and it's possible to find remote positions in other skill areas. I'm interested to see what this list looks like in five to ten years because there will be jobs that didn't even exist when I wrote this book!

Having a skill set, training, or education based in one of the main hard skill areas above can help you determine what types of jobs to pursue. If you don't have hard skills that transfer well to remote work, you might consider developing a skill from the above list, similar to how Kevin did with coding.

Pro Tip: Get Comfortable with Asynchronous Communication

Remote work is shifting the way people communicate. In a traditional office setting, synchronous communication reigns supreme. You stop at Joe's desk to chat about the TPS reports, everyone congregates in the conference room for an all-hands meeting, and you bump into Jane in the hallway to catch up on the past weekend's shenanigans. These are all interactions that provide immediate feedback. Synchronous communication exists in remote work too. It's your conference calls or video sessions.

While synchronous communication is great in an office setting, what happens when you can't have a call? What if half of your colleagues are asleep on the other side of the world while you're working, or when you turn off notifications for a deep work block? How can you possibly get work done as a team?

Cue asynchronous communication. Simply put, asynchronous communication is sending messages without the immediate expectation of a response. This could be an email, Slack message, voice note, or text message. Basically, it would be socially acceptable to respond in minutes, hours, or even days. Having said that, I think many of us have texted with a significant other who would disagree with the premise that you can take days to respond. Oops.

The key to functional asynchronous communication is good writing. Well-written messages can be read and understood without the need to ask for clarification. The key is to do as much as you can with the information available, document what's needed for the next person, and then transfer the ownership of the project via an all-encompassing message to all stakeholders. Asynchronous communication or "async" is about overcommunicating with all vital information and context necessary. If you don't, it can mean significant delays, with time wasted on clarifications.

If you struggle with writing, consider using tools like Grammarly or the Hemingway App. *Everybody Writes* by Ann Handley is a guide for learning how to communicate online effectively. There's also a small book called *The Elements of Style* that contains all of the major grammar rules, but it's as boring as a sack of broken flashlights. If you prefer something more amusing and vulgar, there's *The Elements of F*cking Style*, which is twice as effective because of its humor and crudity.

Professionals who can communicate well asynchronously are increasingly valuable. And just know this, every piece of communication you send, especially to hiring managers and recruiters at remote-first companies, will be scrutinized. So take some time to learn how to write well and communicate across distance, time, and cultures.

Transfer and Upgrade Your Skills

Now that you have a rough idea of what skills companies are looking for, it's time to connect the dots between your abilities and your desired roles.

Set aside some time to reflect on all of the skills you've developed through your life so far. You have had the opportunity to flex at least *some* of the skills covered in this chapter, especially the soft ones. Or you're telling me that in all your life, you've never had to solve a problem, manage your time, or work with others? Even babies fresh out of the womb exhibit great problem-solving skills.

They have a problem, they cry, then they get attention. Don't let a baby beat you on this one.

To best identify your skills, complete the Skills Reflection exercise.

Exercise and Resource: Skills Reflection and Remote Job Search Spreadsheet

Visit www.theremotejobcoach.com/book-resources for the Skills Reflection exercise and the Remote Job Search Spreadsheet, which will help you organize your job search.

After completing the exercise, if you realize you lack some skills right now, don't freak out. It's possible to land (and succeed at) a remote job without having all (or even many) of the skills listed in this chapter. The bigger key is to be growth-minded, willing to learn and to develop competence.

Additionally, by nature, all skills can be practiced. While some skills may come more naturally to you than others, you can get better at any one of them. Identify where you want to get better, and take the action steps to put in the work. You'll likely need to be patient with yourself. Remember, to be good at anything you need to be bad at it first.

If any of the following apply to you, upgrading your skills is a good idea:

- You have no experience working remotely at all, and you're unsure if it's right for you.

- You don't have proficient computer skills, and the digital world doesn't come intuitively.

- You're considering drastic switches in your role or industry and don't have the necessary hard skills.

Now, I'm not here to tell you anything is impossible. I fully support people going after their dreams and making things happen. I mean, shit, if you would've told me when I was younger that I was going to leave the US to travel, work, and live all over the world calling myself The Remote Job Coach, I would've told you it's more likely I'd be a barrelman at a goat rodeo.

If you have less experience, finding a remote job just might take more time and have more steps involved. I've mentioned before that mindset and belief are prerequisites, but it also requires extreme honesty with yourself and knowing your skill level. There's a fine line between needing additional experience or skill development to be competent for the basics of a role, and procrastinating by convincing yourself you need something that you don't actually need to move forward.

Recruiters and hiring managers are looking for people who are a good fit for these roles, so if your skills aren't where they need to be, spend some time bridging the gap. There's plenty you can do to upgrade your skills:

- Find a certification, course, or some type of continuing education in the new niche you're exploring.

- Pitch an internship with an organization or find some way to volunteer your services.

- Find a mentor, coach, or community with particular expertise that can help guide you, provide knowledge, and connect you with other people who are succeeding in that field.

Instead of swimming upstream to try to get a job you're not qualified for, make yourself more qualified. That's exactly what Kevin did, and it's a big reason he was able to succeed working remotely. If you're not willing to put in the work necessary to become more qualified, here's some tough love: remote work is not for you.

You can't expect a remote job to fall into your lap. At the same time, don't feel as if you have to go back and get a new degree to land a remote position. Look for the low-hanging fruit when you pick your first stepping stone. Figure out what's going to most easily get you closer to the life you want to live, and then go after that.

Pro Tip: Be a Specialized Generalist

When it comes to developing skills, there's a lot of debate on what's more valuable: being a specialist or a generalist. Tim Ferriss's YouTube video "Should You Specialize or Be a Generalist?" does a great job of bridging this topic. Here's the thing: at a minimum, you need one marketable hard skill to land a remote position. Logically, though, many people applying for the same positions as you will have the same hard skill. By becoming a *specialized generalist* and combining two or more valuable skills, you can stand out.

When you merge skills in this way, it functions as a multiplier, and the rarer the mix, the better. Tim recommends public speaking, writing, and negotiating as easy, high-value add-ons to a hard skill. Being a data analyst is great, but being a data analyst who is also a great public speaker? Whoa. If you've ever worked in tech, you know the coveted "technical guy who can sell" is a unicorn who gets paid the big bucks. Strive to be unique and valuable! If you focus on only one thing, you have to be *really* good at that thing to stand out. As a specialized generalist, as long as you're pretty good in two or more areas, you can leverage the blend of your skills to bring more to the table.

Use What You've Got and Get What You Need

Bridging the gap between your experience and skills and the job you want is the first major roadblock to overcome in the remote job search. So many people give up at this point. Whether it's due to laziness, lack of confidence, or the wrong priorities, they're not willing to put in the work to develop the skills that will get them their dream remote job. How about you? Think back to your vision. Do you want to spend the next several months or years of your life doing the same shit you know you don't like, or do you want to work toward your vision?

You're reading this book, so I'm going to take a not-so-wild guess and say you want to work toward your vision. Now it's time to follow through. Identify the skills you want to develop and create a plan for doing so. Set aside time every single day to start working toward the dream.

CHAPTER 5

CRANK THE VOLUME

How to Turn Up Your Personal Brand

RUBEN WENT THROUGH A TRAUMATIC EXPERIENCE IN HIS PREVIOUS job, stemming from a conflict with his former management. It was a difficult time in his life that left him frustrated, confused, and ultimately unemployed for almost two years. He did some consulting work to fill in his résumé gap, but nothing was substantial enough to sustain his dream life, which was to travel the world while working remotely.

He was applying to as many remote jobs as he could, many of which he was overqualified for based on his experience level. Left wondering why he couldn't catch a break, he became fixated on obtaining more certifications. He felt that beefing up his credentials would make him more attractive to employers.

After months of taking courses to improve how he looked on paper, he still wasn't getting callbacks. Just having more certifications wasn't helping him tell his story. In addition to that, he still didn't know how to explain the situation with his previous employer in a way that didn't raise concerns. He'd had enough.

I still remember Ruben's first message to me. It read:

I want to be one of your success stories. I will do whatever it takes to get there. It's time! Please let me know how we can get started, your rates, pre-work, or programs I should do. I'm hoping to get one-on-one coaching to fast track me to my goal.

These are the kind of messages I love getting. I knew from day one that Ruben was going to figure it out. From the minute we started working together, he was committed. His passion for learning, absorbing, and then executing was apparent.

I quickly recognized that he didn't have a skills problem, he had a storytelling problem. The way he articulated his personal brand was muddled. I badgered him with a series of questions to pull his story out of him. There are so many valuable bits we tend to forget when we think about ourselves because we're just too close to the situation.

We overhauled his résumé and LinkedIn and developed his brand's voice. We even included a story from his childhood that became a great anecdote to why he developed his skills in his field.

Almost immediately, he started getting attention. I got a text from him a couple of days after we made the changes:

Bro, I just changed my Headline, About Me, photo and banner, and boooom, a recruiter sent me a permanent, 100% remote Process Improvement Analyst position… Ridiculous!

That was just the start. Ruben began getting outreach from recruiters daily. Eventually, he landed a fully remote position with the freedom to travel.

Ruben's story may be similar to yours.

So many job seekers have unconventional backgrounds, dreadful past employment experiences, résumé gaps, or just general apprehension toward describing themselves and their achievements. We grow up in a society that condemns outward signs of self-confidence and trains us to be overly humble.

Yet the entire job search process relies heavily on your ability to brand yourself in a tangible way to get companies to understand your value. You can maintain humility and simultaneously sing your own praises! In this section, we'll go over everything you need to know to crank up the volume on your own personal brand to start getting the attention you deserve.

Change the Input: Reframe Your Mindset

A job search is a direct marketing exercise.

Job searching is all about marketing and sales. You're marketing yourself, your work, and what you can do for an organization. Since you're the product in this situation, put on your empathy hat for employers to understand what you're showcasing to them. Ask yourself the honest truth: If you were them, would you buy the product being presented?! If not, why? This can help you identify places where you're unclear in the marketing of your value. Think about the buying decisions you make on a daily basis. Become more present and aware of the impulses that move you to make purchases. The more you can understand marketing (and sales) at a fundamental level, the better job seeker you'll be.

Everything Starts Online

In the digital age, everything starts online. Dating as a farmer? There's an app for that. Trying a new restaurant but you're risk avoidant? Don't worry, there are millions of "professional" Yelpers on the case. Searching for a remote job? Your first stop: the internet.

Crazy as it seems to me now, I remember recruiting for IBM at my alma mater, Chico State, from 2013 to 2016. We would set up a booth at the job fair and talk to candidates in person. They'd hand us their paper résumés, and we'd have an actual face-to-face conversation. Not to brag, but we also won "Best in Show" at the Business, IT, and SAP career fair in late 2015. I'm like the kid in gym class who tries way too hard to win everything.

While I enjoyed in-person discussions with candidates, the camaraderie between my colleagues and me, and competition with the other booths, these types of fairs aren't meant for remote companies. In fact, there's a whole slew of "virtual job fairs" now specifically meant for remote companies that organizations like FlexJobs, Power to Fly, and WeWorkRemotely put on.

All this to say, finding a remote job requires you to be "good at the internet." And it benefits you because interacting with companies online is far more scalable than anything you can do in person.

Hiring managers and recruiters, when looking for qualified candidates to fill a position, are leveraging online tools: job boards, applicant tracking systems, and their networks on LinkedIn. It just makes sense for you to go where these companies are already searching so you can be found.

Whether you like it or not, your online identity is becoming just as much of a representation of you as, well, you. Virtual and augmented reality, the metaverse, NFTs, and crypto are all examples of how innovation in the digital space creates opportunities to live more of our lives in a digital world instead of in "reality."

At some point, we'll not only be doing remote job interviews in the metaverse but company happy hours will be at virtual bars that your "avatar" can stumble out of. Team meetings will be held in virtualized conference rooms where everyone's characters are sitting there looking bored, likely pulling out their simulated cell phones and texting under tables, just like you'd do in person.

Right now, the main scrutiny of your online profile when it comes to a remote job is what you have on LinkedIn. In the future, it may be some profile you create to represent yourself within the metaverse. Who knows?

The point is, your personal brand establishes your credibility, determines the opportunities available to you, and can influence an employer's desire to hire you. For this reason, learning how to cultivate a personal brand and use it to your advantage is one of the most important investments to make in your remote job search.

Pro Tip: Use a Word Cloud to Curate Keywords for Your Brand

When a company is looking to fill a position, they search based on their desired keywords. If you're not using their words, you're not going to be found. By speaking their language, you're more likely to be hired.

Look at five to ten job descriptions for roles similar to what you're looking for. Then feed them into a word cloud generator (Google "word cloud generator," and you'll get lots of free options). That will show you the most-used words across all the job descriptions. Take those keywords and incorporate them into your profiles, résumés, and personal brand strategy.

What's Your Personal Brand?

You already have a personal brand, and you use it all the time. Think about it ... every day you present yourself in a certain way through the clothes you wear, the things you buy, what you post to your social media accounts, and so on. All of these actions contribute to your personal brand. In my definition of a personal brand, I came up with an easy equation:

$$(\text{Your Self-Image} + \text{Others' Perception}) \times \text{Behavior} = \text{Personal Brand}$$

Your self-image is how you see yourself—who you think you are and who you *want* to be. Your self-image is intuitive and comes from self-awareness.

Others' perception is also self-explanatory: it's how other people see you. If you have strong self-awareness, you probably already have some idea of how people see you, but it's safe to assume you've got some blind spots. To know what people think of you, ask. In *The Miracle Morning*, Hal Elrod suggests sending an email to the people closest to you to ask them targeted questions that will help you get an understanding of what other people see. I recommend doing a similar exercise. Choose a handful of people who know you well and whom you trust. These need to be people who also won't bullshit you. Ask their opinion of what your three greatest strengths and three greatest weaknesses (or areas of improvement) are. You might be surprised by what you learn.

Last and most important is your behavior. People will judge you the most based on what you do, not what you say, which is why your behavior is a multiplier in the personal brand equation. A lot of people overlook their behavior online because of its separation from the "real world." This is a huge mistake. It's how some poor souls become hate-filled trolls that incite conspiracy theories on dark web message boards with anonymous burner accounts, all while in the comfort of their mother's basement.

How you act online should be akin to how you act in person. The closer you can align the two, the more your values and personality will shine through. This doesn't mean oversharing, but it means understanding that potential employers can see a record of your activity: posts, comments, and even likes. So be careful of the minefield that is your social media feed. What you engage with, whether one errant like on a controversial post or a random comment battle with your uncle about politics, becomes the reflection of you that everyone else gets to see. Wouldn't it be wise to influence that narrative in an authentic way that helps instead of harms you?

Exercise: Safeguarding Your Online Reputation

One of the first things prospective employers will do is Google you. Being aware of what they will find can help you better cultivate your brand. Visit www.theremotejobcoach.com/book-resources for an exercise to assess your online reputation, along with some extra tips on how to clean it up if necessary.

What's the right brand look like? Well, that depends entirely on you. There's no one-size-fits-all answer here. Connect back to You 2.0 (from chapter 2). What would this person's brand look like?

The goal is to get a job, so appealing to potential employers and showing your talent and value is key. But the goal isn't to get *any* job; it's to get the right remote job for you that's going to improve your overall life.

Authenticity will help connect you to companies and jobs that are the right fit. Ultimately, your brand is your story, and you're the one best positioned to write it. Consciously cultivate it so your self-image, others' perception, and your behavior are all aligned to reflect who you want to be.

Digital Proximity: Master the Art of the "Pull"

Think back to a crush you had as a kid. You probably did some dumb shit to get them to notice you, right? Maybe you awkwardly walked past their locker a dozen times a day even though it was completely out of your way, or joined a club you had no interest in because you knew they were a part of it. You came up with excuses to put yourself in their general vicinity. That's exactly what to do with employers, minus the discomfort of prepubescent clumsiness. It's your responsibility to put yourself in a position to be discovered. You can do this by creating what I call a *platform for digital proximity*.

Your platform is all of your digital assets—social media profiles, content you've created, website, and so on. When you design your platform for *digital proximity*, you're intentional about creating your digital assets in the same spaces as the companies you want to work for. You're wedging your digital foot in the door and giving yourself a chance to open it.

In the job search process, you'll be engaging in "push" and "pull" strategies. "Push" (also known as "outbound") activities are when you are doing all the work to push the awareness of your skills and interest to the companies you're interested in. Here's what that looks like:

- You reach out to employers/hiring managers.

- You apply for positions online and send out your résumé.

- You try to provide your credentials or social proof through explanation.

The beauty and art of the "pull" (or "inbound") strategy is that instead of chasing after the companies you want to work for, you create reasons for them to come to you. A pull strategy, if done effectively, looks like this:

- Hiring managers, employers, or recruiters reach out to you.

- Friends see an opening at their company and immediately think of submitting your résumé for you.

- Potential hiring managers find your social proof online through your recommendations and personal branding.

In the job search, both push and pull strategies are valuable, but the more you can pull employers to you, the better. Not only will it save you time and energy, but it shifts the dynamic of leverage. Instead of you trying to convince a company to hire you, the company is trying to convince you to come work for them.

The techniques that follow in this section are ways to build a platform for proximity and become a magnet for opportunities. As an added bonus, you can also use these things in your push strategies, linking them in materials you send to companies to help prove your value.

These suggestions might be foreign, new, and even the idea of them may feel awkward. Remember, anything worth doing is going to be uncomfortable at first. Be patient with yourself. The idea isn't to go and do everything in this section all at once. Nothing in this section is "mandatory." It's here to give you options and help you understand the techniques you can use to create longevity in your personal brand, so you continue to attract the right types of people toward you.

VIDEO CONTENT

Whatever your niche is, there are ways to use your expertise to educate others. According to Cisco, video makes up over 80% of all content consumed, so it's the perfect medium. Anyone has the ability to post videos on a wide variety of social platforms: YouTube, Instagram, Facebook, LinkedIn, Vimeo, and so on.

My friend and video content strategist Fanny Dunagan recommends:

- Find a job description you want to apply to.

- Pick out key bullet points from the job responsibilities you have expertise in.

- Create videos around that expertise.

It's simple, and over time, you build a collection of videos showcasing your skills. Not only will these videos demonstrate your expertise, but they humanize and create a 3D version of you. When you create videos, people feel like they know you before they meet you.

PERSONAL WEBSITE

Companies want to know the person behind the computer. Having a website that shows who you are can give you a supreme advantage. People will judge you using the narrative available to them. Your goal is to influence the narrative in the way you want your story to be told. If you don't tell your own story, who's going to?

It's easy to create a personal website, so there's no excuse not to have one if you want one. With cheap templates and hosting sites, you can easily show off your skills, expertise, and portfolio.

For a website, my recommendation is to include at a minimum:

- Relevant portfolio (especially for designers and creatives)

- About me / summary (a paragraph setting your intention and high level of what you're looking for or the industry you're interested in)

- Background (an online résumé)

- Contact info (at least a way to contact you through the site)

- Something that shows your personality and interests (e.g., a photo of you someplace interesting, details about your hobbies, and other conversation starters)

Building a successful remote company relies heavily on investment in team culture. The more you can show you'd be a good organizational fit for a company, the more likely they'll hire you, and a website is a great way to do that.

BLOGS AND SOCIAL MEDIA POSTS

Remember when I said writing is the most valuable skill you can cultivate? Well, here's your chance to show it off! If you create a website, consider also adding a blog that serves to educate and show your expertise in topics relevant to your remote job search.

If you don't want to create a blog, that's okay too. You could write as a contributor or a guest blogger for other blogs and publications. You can also use a free blogging platform like Medium if you don't have a website.

I also recommend posting on the social media platform(s) of your choice. For most people reading this, LinkedIn is the best place to publish professional-related content. Regardless of platform, the most important part of posting is your intentionality, comfortability with the platform(s) you choose, and consistency.

As of this writing, only about 1% of LinkedIn's eight hundred million users share content weekly. This is why I love LinkedIn for job seekers. By being part of that small percentage, you automatically stand out and increase your chances of virtually "bumping into" the right people.

Here are a few ways to easily post online without needing to fully create something new:

- Reshare someone else's article or post you like with your own perspective attached.

- If you wrote a blog, repurpose snippets of it as individual posts.

- Find old projects or work samples that can be converted into learnings for your audience.

The point is to use social media strategically. Remember, you're trying to create assets that highlight your expertise to potential employers. Imagine you're a developer applying to a remote dev job, and the hiring manager searches your name, and an article on a developer-specific blog pops up. If I were a hiring manager, and assuming your posts are helpful, you stand out immediately.

PUBLIC SPEAKING

Research from RH Bruskin states that public speaking is the number one fear for most people, even more than death. If you fall into that category, then this could be an opportunity for you to get over your fear, majorly improve your communication skills, and increase your stock as a candidate. If you already enjoy public speaking, even better.

Speaking doesn't have to be a huge, nerve-wracking experience, and often you can ease your way into it. Start with a small audience, a short talk, or something virtual. The important thing is to put yourself out there.

Public speaking is a skill, and the more you practice, the better you'll get at communicating. You might not be donning a black turtleneck and giving grandiose presentations like Steve Jobs, but if you find yourself needing to share your opinion in front of even a small group of colleagues on team calls, for instance, speaking experience can serve you well. It also gets you prepared for interviews and helps you build confidence. Yes, you might want to highlight your public speaking as social proof of your qualifications, but the real value is in the increased ability to display competence in your communication with others.

Resource: Public Speaking Guide

Visit www.theremotejobcoach.com/book-resources for a guide on public speaking, with tips on where to find public speaking opportunities and strategies for structuring your talk.

Creative expression is one of the largest missed opportunities for job seekers available. All of these strategies are great ways to show your expertise and build your brand while also expressing yourself. Find the ways that are most natural for you but don't be afraid to stretch your comfort zone and share your proficiencies. You never know who will find it.

LinkedIn Is Your Landing Page

LinkedIn is the Swiss Army knife for your remote job search and career, helping you find job listings, message and connect with decision makers, and communicate your personal brand to the world. Here are some compelling LinkedIn statistics (pulled from 2020 and 2022 data):

- More than fifty-five million companies are listed on LinkedIn with millions of open jobs every month.

- 87% of recruiters regularly use LinkedIn to assist in their hiring efforts.

- On LinkedIn, seventy-seven job applications are submitted every second and six people are hired every minute.

- Of active LinkedIn users, sixty-one million are senior-level influencers, and sixty-five million decision makers.

- LinkedIn makes up more than 50% of all social traffic to B2B websites and blogs.

- LinkedIn is the most used social media among Fortune 500 companies.

Everyone will look at your LinkedIn profile: hiring managers, recruiters, decision makers, potential colleagues. It's your job to influence what they see.

A landing page, as defined by Hubspot, is "a specific page on your website where you collect a visitor's contact information in exchange for a resource." The page is designed to encourage a specific action from the visitor.

That's why I say LinkedIn is your landing page. It's where you have a limited amount of space to fit all the information anyone needs to know about you to make a decision whether or not to engage. It's your opportunity to tell the story of you, so make it a damn compelling one.

For most people I've worked with, the most commonly neglected parts of their remote job search both deal with LinkedIn:

- Optimizing their profile for success

- Using the platform to network efficiently

Based on my experiences, revamping your profile and learning how to connect with others are the two most bang-for-your-buck activities that provide the greatest and quickest ROI. The key is to overhaul your LinkedIn profile and usage based on who you want to be in the future, not just who you've been in the past. Remember *be, do, have*?

Be One of a Kind

Remote positions are open to a wider pool of candidates, so you're likely going to be competing against more applicants than a locally based role. One of the biggest struggles for job seekers is differentiating themselves. They apply online, send in a standard résumé, and sit on their hands and wait for a response like 90%+ of the others. Is there any wonder why they don't get a reply? By doing the exact same thing as everyone else, they look exactly like everyone else, and they get the exact same result.

The key to finding success, especially with your target company or dream remote job, is looking different, not the same. With the strategies and tips from this chapter, you can create a brand that differentiates you and puts you within the top percentile of job applicants just by the nature of being unique and catching the company's attention.

CHAPTER 6

EXPLORE THE MENU

Know How to Find Legit Remote Jobs

MELODIE WAS OUT OF WORK, SO SHE SAT DOWN AND CREATED A LIST of everything she wanted in her dream job. At the time she was living in Bali, Indonesia, but her parents, who were living in the United States, were getting older and she needed the flexibility to travel back and take care of them at the drop of a hat. Working remotely was her solution.

She began her search and quickly grew frustrated. Melodie had a clear vision for the role she wanted, but it didn't seem to exist when she looked at job listings. She worked in a niche industry (biotech) as a chief of staff, and most chief of staff positions weren't remote. She had decades of experience, but wasn't getting any positive responses. Doubt crept into her mind. Maybe a remote position wasn't in the cards for her. While she had the skills, people sometimes assumed she couldn't do certain things because she was more senior. Due to this ageism, she was passed over for several opportunities.

After we started working together, I encouraged her to begin networking on LinkedIn and exchanging messages with people. She slowly built real, legitimate relationships. She would listen to podcasts and reach out to the hosts to suggest episode ideas, offering creative contributions that were meaningful to them. She also pitched herself as a volunteer to help companies involved in COVID-19 relief efforts and research. By volunteering ten to twenty hours a week, she was able to stay in the rhythm of working and avoid gaps in her résumé, while simultaneously proving her value, strengthening her industry relationships, and supporting a cause she believed in.

Eventually, within five months of meeting one of her connections, she received some contract work from him. Because she excelled in that gig, he ended up recommending her for a position at a small biotech company. The company didn't interview anyone else, and after one telephone call, they offered her the job. The best part? The position checked off nearly everything on her dream job list.

In any job search, your ability to get the right job is limited by your ability to find and attract opportunities while simultaneously proving you're the best fit. After talking with thousands of job seekers, I've devised a set of best practices for finding the right job opportunities in a creative, yet efficient way. This methodology is your way of exploring the menu and discovering what's out there.

Start with Companies, Not Job Boards

Most job seekers start their search (and focus most of their efforts) scanning through endless tabs of job boards. They put their metaphorical hands out, asking the job board gods to bless them with a relevant role that fits what they're looking for.

The problem is, *starting* with job boards is reactive. When you find random listings on job boards, they often take you down rabbit holes of idealization. You might get excited because you finally found a remote job that looks like a perfect fit! You spend the rest of the day taking hours to curate your materials. You customize your résumé, create a cover letter, and answer the application questions. Finally, after pressing submit, you breathe a sigh of relief. You feel good about this one.

A week later you get an email to set up an interview. Wow! This is the one, you knew it! You set up the call with the recruiter and you couldn't be more elated. The anxious excitement builds, and it's finally the day of the screening. You jump on with the recruiter, ready to rock it, and you do. The first call was a quick one, and you did enough to get passed onto the next step. Now you're really flying high.

In the next interview you're set to meet the hiring manager. You're a bit more nervous for this one and know you gotta bring the big guns. You've practiced your stories, you've looked over your résumé a hundred times, and you've even got a nice cheat sheet on your screen that you can reference. Nothing is going to stop you. The hiring manager jumps on, and after exchanging some pleasantries, he drops the bomb on you.

The company is making plans to go back to the office. This job will not be fully remote. It's mandatory to go into the office at least three times a week. Fully remote work was only temporary because of the pandemic, and they're asking all candidates to be willing to relocate. You feel your stomach drop as if you were riding a roller coaster, and you drop out of the process.

This happened to one of my clients prior to working with me, and you'd be surprised how common this problem is. Since the term "remote work" can indicate a wide variety of circumstances, it's essential to get clarification, especially from companies you're interested in working for, exactly what their version of "remote" actually means. Their beliefs about remote work and the intentionality in which they use it shapes their policies, culture, and ultimately the support you receive as an employee.

Instead of heading straight to job boards, by starting with companies—researching and creating a list of remote companies you want to work for—you ensure you're only expending effort on the types of organizations that can give you the lifestyle you desire. You'll minimize the chances of taking the wrong job or wasting time applying to a company where you'll have to negotiate the terms of your flexibility, or have the rug pulled on you.

Select Companies to Target

A job search for a graphic designer from the United States who wants to work from home in Arkansas and a job search for a sales specialist from Indonesia whose goal is to travel through Latin America are going to be notably different. (I'm describing two of my past, successful clients, by the way.) The types of companies available to provide each of them with their ideal lifestyle are distinct, thus their search strategies need to be distinct as well.

Exercise: Target Companies Worksheet

Visit www.theremotejobcoach.com/book-resources for a worksheet version of the following questions on how to select your company criteria and brainstorm companies to target.

Earlier in the book, you visualized your ideal lifestyle and reflected on your past experiences. Use these parameters to guide you in choosing selection criteria for the type of company you want to work for. Getting extremely clear on each of these is crucial to your success.

Here are a few ideas on how to select criteria for companies. Get as specific as you can. That way, when you use filters to try to search for them, you get a list that's manageable. Think of the ideal situation:

- What industry is the company in? Try to get down to one or two at the most!

- What size is the organization?

- What types of benefits do they offer?

- How do they describe their culture?

- What kinds of causes are important to the company?

- How "remote" are they, and what is their sentiment about remote work?

- Where do they hire?

- How are they innovating, or what are they creating?

- [Add your own criteria question here]

Once you have these answered, it's time to look for companies that fit your criteria! Don't go down wormholes at this stage. To start your brainstorming, make a large list first, knowing you can cut it down later. Think about the following and start writing these companies down:

- Which companies are top of mind that you admire or want to work at?

- Which companies make products or services you're aligned with or use frequently?

- Which companies serve the market you're interested in?

- Which companies are innovating or growing in their industry?

- Which companies create something that won't bore you to death and that you actually might be passionate about?

- Which companies do you know people that work there and love it?

- [Add your own criteria question here]

After answering those, you can also do things like:

- Search for "round-up" articles, like "Top [Industry] Remote Companies."

- Look at awarded companies, like the FlexJobs Top 100.

- Find companies you like on LinkedIn, and look on the right-hand side where it says "similar companies."

- Sort on job boards by the filters you've established (especially the type of remote and industry) and take note of what companies come up even if there are no jobs for your role.

At this point you should have a healthy list of companies. You can begin to narrow down this broad list by doing research on each individual company to determine which actually seem aligned to your preferences. Your goal is to use this list as an important resource for your search, so make sure you're constantly updating it.

Change the Input: Reframe Your Mindset

The most qualified candidates aren't always chosen.

In a world with intense competition for remote positions, the highest, most qualified candidates are being left behind. Why? Because the people who get the jobs are not always the ones who look the best on paper. Organizations in remote environments need employees with strong EQ (emotional intelligence) and soft skills, so they hire those who articulate their value, package their experience the right way, and build trust (and become someone the employer likes and wants to work with).

This is good and bad news, depending on how you look at it. The bad news is you can't rely on your qualifications alone to get your position. The good news is you don't have to worry about being the *best* or *perfect* candidate. There will always be someone more qualified than you, especially when competing on a global scale for remote positions. Fortunately, there are other ways to get noticed and articulate your value to employers.

When searching for job opportunities, if you don't feel 100% qualified, go for it anyway! With the lessons in this book, you'll be able to stand out and might land your dream job even if you aren't technically the most qualified candidate.

Use Job Boards Effectively

Job boards enable you to view, evaluate, and submit applications to many positions quickly. While that can feel productive, it's deceptive. Often, you're not actually making the progress you think you are, because there's no correlation between the number of applications you submit and the number of interviews you receive as a result. Remember, we're going for quality over quantity. I've had some people come to me after applying to over five hundred jobs without getting a single interview, and I've had clients of mine get a job without applying to any jobs at all.

Does this mean you shouldn't use job boards? No. While utilizing job boards shouldn't be your only—or even primary—activity in your job search, they do serve a purpose as a *supplement*. My recommendation is to use them to:

1. Create an *inbound* lead flow of new opportunities and find companies you can target

2. Research remote roles and descriptions for your keywords

3. Supplement a well-rounded search that prioritizes building relationships and branding

First, there are hundreds if not thousands of job boards out there. You'll drive yourself crazy if you try to use *all* of them. Instead, figure out which ones are most relevant for your particular situation, and dive deep into those. I would narrow it down to the top three to five that are most valuable to your needs.

Rather than wasting a bunch of time searching job boards everyday, automate this process as much as possible. That's what I mean when I say *inbound*. The best job boards have extreme levels of customization and alert functionality to send the most relevant stuff straight to your inbox. Use this to your advantage so you're as efficient as possible. Set up alerts for your particular search, be as specific as possible, and segment a limited amount of time each week to skim the most recent postings. Don't just apply for every somewhat relevant position you see either. If you see a job that might fit, don't forget to do your research on the company first. Then, if you determine you're aligned with the company, make time to strategize how you can find a sponsor in the organization and be unique in your application process (I'll show you how in the next few chapters). The extra effort you spend upfront at this stage ultimately saves you work in the long run.

This level of intentionality is lost on most job seekers. Without it, you can get lost in job boards, sinking hours and hours rummaging through sites like they're discount bins at the thrift store.

Think of it in terms of the Pareto principle, also known as the 80-20 rule, which says 80% of outcomes come from 20% of all causes. To get the highest return on your time and efforts, find the 20% of job search activities that will yield you 80% of the results. In the job search, that means focusing on proactive strategies, like networking and branding yourself for your target companies, not spending all your effort and energy on job boards.

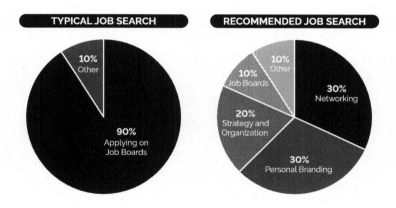

Resource: Find Remote Jobs For You

Visit www.theremotejobcoach.com/book-resources for the Find Remote Jobs for You resource, which includes a curated list of job boards, including location- and industry-specific ones, and remote job communities.

Focus Based on Your Priorities

At this point you've reflected on your motivations for working remotely, the types of jobs you're qualified for, and which types of companies to target. You know your priorities. Tailoring your search strategy based on these priorities will help you get the most return on investment. Knowing your specific circumstances, your ideal situation, and the resources available, where does it make sense to focus your time and energy?

In the following table I describe examples of various priorities you may have and some of my recommended, corresponding search strategies. Note that you may have competing priorities, and one of these may not be your clear number one. That's totally fine. This is meant to give you a jumping-off point and ideas of how you can incorporate various high-level tactics into a comprehensive plan. You'll recognize some of these strategies from earlier in the book, and others will be explained in the coming chapters.

Priority	Search Strategies
Industry: The specific industry is most important to you (e.g., biotech, SaaS, etc.).	Search for organizations in this industry that fit your company criteria.
	Connect with people you already know in that industry.
	Join industry-specific communities to expand your network.
	Find employees in this industry and reach out for informational interviews.
	Engage with and create content about the industry you're interested in.
	Filter job boards for your chosen industry and set specific alerts.

Priority	Search Strategies
Job Role: The specific role is most important to you (i.e., you have a specific skill set or role you're specialized in).	Reach out to people you already know doing that role. Join role-specific communities to expand your network. Find employees at your target organizations that have this role and reach out for informational interviews. Engage with and create content about tasks specific to this role. Filter job boards for your chosen role and set specific alerts.
Travel: The job giving you the freedom and ability to travel is the most important.	Focus on "all-remote" or "remote-first" companies with "Work from Anywhere" policies. Get in touch with people you already know working at these types of companies. Join digital nomad communities to expand your network. Find employees at these companies and reach out for informational interviews. Filter job boards for "Work from Anywhere" opportunities and set your alerts. Consider freelancing, as it offers more freedom than many remote jobs.

Priority	Search Strategies
Money: Making a certain amount of money is the most important thing for you.	Focus on bigger companies with larger budgets and more stability to pay higher wages. (Also ensure you have the skills and role type to command a higher salary.) Check various transparent compensation sites to see which companies hiring remotely have salary data to reference. Connect with those you know working remotely for a large corporation. Find employees at these companies and reach out for informational interviews. Filter job boards for higher-salary positions and set specific alerts.
Variety: Having variety in your experience as well as less structure and the ability to wear multiple hats is your biggest priority.	Focus on smaller companies and startups, where there tends to be more dynamic change and different responsibilities available. Connect with people you already know working at these types of companies. Join startup communities to expand your network. Find employees at these companies and reach out for informational interviews. Filter job boards for startups and set specific alerts.

Priority	Search Strategies
Company: You know which company you want to work for, and that's your highest priority.	Evaluate who you already know that works there or who knows someone that works there.
	Join the company's virtual events and communities if applicable.
	Find employees at the company you can relate to in some way and reach out for informational interviews.
	Follow the company on all social media and subscribe to their communications.
	Engage with the company content and with employees at the organization.
	Create content about the company in a meaningful way.
	Become a customer of the company's services or products if applicable.
	Set up alerts on Google for the organization.

You'll notice that the fundamental strategies are similar, simply customized to the priority. Regardless of your priorities, starting with a targeted company approach and an intense focus on networking are both key components to any success, no matter what your specific goal is. These lists are not exhaustive; they're meant to help you reframe your mindset and figure out what you might start doing to create opportunities that don't involve just going on job boards and applying. We'll go into more detail in later chapters about how to build trust, apply in a unique way, and execute many of these techniques in a more comprehensive fashion.

Beware of Scams

Like the catfishers who pose as internet models to get their phone bills paid, or the Instagrammers who can't stop DMing me about forex opportunities, the remote job industry is filled with scams.

There will always be people in this world preying upon others. According to a data report from Bromium, social media cyber crimes generate global revenue that tops $3.25 billion annually as of 2020. Only a portion of this amount comes from work-from-home scams, but the point is, it's a profitable business to scam you.

Many of these scams will promise remote work with ease. Flexible hours, high pay, little work, and even free back massages. Well, maybe the back massages were only promised by the catfish I left on read. Either way, the truth is, the *best* remote jobs, the *legit* ones with awesome remote-first companies, not only require a fair amount of work, but they are also extremely competitive to obtain.

You'll save yourself a lot of time (and, potentially, money too) if you know how to spot online work-from-home scams. Here are some red flags that indicate a "job" is likely a scam:

- **Work from home is highlighted as the main part of the title.** If the *main* focus of a job is the fact that it allows you to work from home or remotely, it's something to be cautious of. Especially watch out if the job title is about working from home and doesn't mention a role name, like "Work from Home Job Making $X per Week." Most legitimate job roles focus on the role title itself, rather than the fact it's a work-from-home job. There's also usually a separate area in the listing for a company to classify the location as remote, so it's not needed as such a prominent part of the title unless they are trying to lure people in who are desperate.

- **It sounds too good to be true.** Incredible perks, insane salary for little or no work hours, or any other vague but irrational claims are a huge red flag. Their goal here is to entice you. It would be great if you could make multiple thousands in a day with no skills required beyond scrolling on your phone, but if it sounds too good to be true, it probably is.

- **There's a lack of information available.** If the job description is vague with only a few words and you have to have a call with a member from their organization or submit your information to learn more, it's usually either an MLM or some type of scam. While MLMs aren't necessarily always scams, be wary of anything that falls into the realm of a pyramid scheme. Do your research. In a lot of cases, a kid could make more running a lemonade stand than the average MLM salesperson makes in a year.

- **The opportunity came from a vague post in an internet group or forum.** Communities on Facebook and LinkedIn can be helpful, but the quality of remote jobs posted in some of these groups can be lower and less reliable than other sources. Since you're less able to qualify or filter what you see, it's often random, and there's frequently a higher prevalence of scams. Many people who prey on others will target such communities by posting something vague and requiring you to DM them for more info. Don't dismiss all opportunities from these groups, but examine them closely.

- **You're asked for personal info or money upfront.** You shouldn't be expected to pay someone money upfront for a job. If they require an initial investment, be extremely cautious and skeptical of the opportunity.

- **It doesn't feel right.** Sometimes all you need is your intuition to tell you something isn't right. If you get a bad feeling inside that something is wrong with a company, you may be right. Trust yourself and do additional research before becoming more involved.

- **You received an email from someone unknown with mysterious links.** Getting cold emails from people you don't know is cause for caution, especially if the email has a link in it. These tend to be phishing scams, where the sender is trying to get you to click the link, which can cause problems on your computer or take you to a site that asks you to submit more personal information. Don't click on these links. Mark the email as spam or phishing, and block the user.

- **The website is non-secure.** Be aware if a website is using HTTP instead of HTTPS. HTTPS is a secure communication over a computer network, widely used, and trusted. Unsecured sites without the *S* may have the potential to be harmful.

- **There's a strange sense of urgency.** If an offer is time-sensitive and you're being rushed (e.g., they tell you a job offer is about to expire), the interview process is weirdly accelerated, or they're putting pressure on you, it could be a potential scam.

- **There are spelling/grammar errors.** Scammers care more about money than grammar. Many times they may not speak English as a first language, so look out for misspelled words and incorrect sentence structure. These could be warning signs.

When in doubt, *research*! Look the company up on credible websites. Try to find them on LinkedIn, the Better Business Bureau, Glassdoor, and Google. If you've been given an individual's name, look them up on LinkedIn. You can even search "[name of company] + scam" to see if other people online are talking about their negative experiences. Trust your intuition and be cautious.

Pro Tip: Consider Doing Pro Bono Work

If you're struggling to find job opportunities, consider doing pro bono project-based work. This is a great way to gain experience and offset skill gaps, and it might even lead to paid opportunities. If you go this route, seek to earn testimonials, and work with people who have experience either in your industry or in leading and working with people in your role, so you can learn from them and develop your skills.

There's a misconception that free work is automatically valuable to a corporation. While they may not be paying you, you still require investment, in time and energy, to manage. Volunteers often take *more* work to manage, because they tend to be less reliable than paid employees and may not produce the same quality of work. Because of this, from the company's perspective, accepting free work is not necessarily easy or appealing—or safe! There's a legal liability in allowing people to see internal company data. While volunteer work can be a great way to fill out your résumé and open up future job opportunities, companies won't be lining up. It's your responsibility to make a compelling case.

You Can Find Legitimate, Well-Paying Remote Positions

Legitimate, well-paying remote positions at awesome companies *are* out there. Finding them takes more intention than most job seekers are used to. By reimagining how you conduct a job search, you'll have a much better chance of finding a remote position that gets you closer to your ideal vision of freedom.

Of everything you can do, the strategy with the greatest ROI is *networking*. Learning how to build relationships and leverage your connections will have a huge impact on your remote job search.

CHAPTER 7

ON-DEMAND

Networking is the Shortcut to What You Want

KELLY WAS BURNED OUT AFTER MANY YEARS IN A CHAOTIC WORK environment. She had a decade of high-performing sales experience in the media and advertising space, but because of the toxicity in her workplace, she'd lost confidence in herself and doubted she'd be able to transfer her experience to a new industry. She didn't want a change; she *needed* a change.

We began working together, and after rebuilding how she presented her skills on LinkedIn, she found a role that excited her. The company was a high-growth videoconferencing start-up in the tech field that offered remote flexibility.

She looked within her network and discovered she knew someone who knew someone at the company. I also had a close contact who worked there in the same role she was interested in. I reached out to the person I knew, and Kelly asked her friend to connect her with their contact.

Before even applying, she had two informational interviews, which she used to get inside information about the organization, the culture, and the position. She liked the high growth potential, and the work culture was a complete 180 from her current position. The people who worked for this company actually enjoyed working there. That was a foreign concept to her at the time.

The next Monday, when she went to officially apply, the role had been taken down. She freaked out. "Oh my god. We waited too long," she said. "I missed my chance." Then she asked, "What should I do?"

During the informational interviews, she'd received the hiring manager's direct contact information. I told her to send him an email explaining the situation and to include all the materials we'd created: a customized cover letter, résumé, and video (which she used their platform to record), all directed toward this hiring manager. She led with what she'd learned from her conversations with the other employees, which showed her proactivity.

Her application also came wrapped in the best packaging: social proof. The hiring manager knew—and trusted—who she got his contact info from, and these people were vouching for Kelly.

Within twenty-four hours, a recruiter reached out to schedule an interview, and she ended up being hired for a position that hadn't even been posted yet. Kelly landed the position in only five weeks. How's that for being unique?

Long after her hiring, the manager still commented on how impressed he was with her ability to navigate the organization from outside of it. And since her role was in sales, she proved her ability to do the job through the application process.

Networking is like the on-demand button on your remote. By knowing where you want to go, you can shortcut the process. Networking isn't always easy, and not all referrals are created equal, but if you make a concerted effort to focus your energy on building relationships, your life and the opportunities available to you will change completely.

Networking = Your Solution to Any Challenge

Whatever challenge you have, networking is your solution. Need more clients? Network better. Looking for a significant other or friends? Network better. Want more job opportunities? Network better. Your ability to interact with others and navigate social dynamics with emotional intelligence is the biggest indicator of life success, happiness, and fulfillment.

CAREER SUCCESS

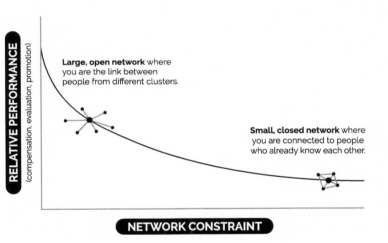

Whatever your thoughts are on networking, you're already doing it. Networking simply describes the interconnected web of human interaction we're all part of. Relationships are the core of everything we do, and getting good at networking just means getting good at making friends. I use the terms "networking" and "building relationships" interchangeably because they mean the same thing to me. In the context of job searching, our aim is to be more intentional with how you build relationships so that they can support you in achieving your remote life goals.

Networking has been the single most impactful strategy I've used to get what I want out of my career. My mentor in university was the one who got me my interview at IBM. When I landed my job at a small PR firm while living in Portland, Oregon, I didn't formally apply. I'd met the founder at a Forbes 30 Under 30 conference in Boston, and she randomly texted me asking if I knew someone for a role. That someone was me. Working for Remote Year was much of the same. I did the program as a customer, networked with their employees, told them about my intentions to work there, showed them why I was a great fit, and ultimately my résumé was submitted for me by two different people once they had a job open.

Most jobs that get filled are influenced in some way by preexisting relationships. When someone at a company vouches for you, that trust is transferred. Many people use LinkedIn's "Easy Apply" in their job search, but the irony is that it's not easier in the long run. Especially if your résumé isn't absolutely perfect for the job, it only makes *applying* easier, not getting an interview easier. *Rather than focusing on the easiest way to submit an application, focus on how to make yourself the easiest hiring decision for the company.* To do that, relationship building is your best bet.

Bottom line: To get hired the difficult way, apply online. To get hired the easy way, network.

Everybody has a network already, and within the people you already know are potential introductions, job opportunities, and advice that can help you get to the next level. But networks vary in quality. The measure of your network is its power and ability to provide you with the opportunities you desire.

Your network will be most effective if you consciously and consistently build it over time, forming connections with people who work at companies you admire, have expertise in the niche you're interested in, or can otherwise be a net positive in your life.

The goal of networking when it comes to job seeking is threefold:

- Identify and build relationships with the kind of people who either do what you do or hire people who do what you do

- Show decision makers you're competent, creative, and persistent

- Position yourself as the only option in the company's mind

But, like everything we're talking about in this book, networking takes effort. If you're not willing to play the long game when building your network, you'll always act in shortsighted, self-serving ways, and people will avoid you like a plague. Here's an easy formula for networking success:

$$(Intention + Value) \times Consistency = Results$$

Having a pure *intention* sets the tone. If you're only in this to take opportunities from others and manipulate people into doing what you want, eventually folks will figure you out. Being genuine goes a long way.

We'll go into more depth about the second component of the formula, *value*, in this chapter. For now, just consider how others perceive you. Are you a valuable asset to them in their network? Or are you a leech they can't wait to get rid of?

Last but not least, *consistency* becomes the multiplier for your progress and the most important way to compound your network's growth. If you show up day after day as a valuable asset to your network with the right intention, everything will change for you.

The strategies in this section will be like gasoline to a fire if you've had any prior momentum with networking. If you've done a poor job building relationships in your life up to this point, it doesn't mean you should give up hope, but you're required to start intentionally building your network, *now*. Action now means mobility and opportunity later, and our goal is to always put you in a position where you have future choices.

Common Networking Mistakes

Often, when people tell me they hate networking, or they're bad at it, I find the problem is they've just never learned how to do it. That leads to angst when starting conversations, embarrassment when reaching out, and nerves about how others might view them. They overthink it so much it paralyzes them into doing nothing, which is far worse than the non-lethal dose of social anxiety required to take action. Let's go through a list of common networking mistakes I see constantly.

1. **Only networking when you need something.** Time and time again, someone will totally neglect building their network, and then all of a sudden they need a job. They scramble to make up for lost time, but it comes from a place of scarcity and desperation. Instead of interacting in a low-pressure situation asking for help from people they've already built a foundation with, everyone they reach out to is a stranger. Since you're reading this book, I'm guessing you're actively searching for a job, and there's a good chance you haven't been as intentional with your networking as you could be. It's not the end of the world, but be aware that you have ground to make up, and strive to be more consistent with your efforts moving forward. Dig your well before you're thirsty!

2. **Only being interested in what you can get, not what you can give.** No one likes a taker. You know the type. We all have someone in our life who, every time they reach out, asks for something. It could be money, resources, advice, or time. It's frustrating how predictable they can be with their selfishness, and their constant requests without consideration signify low emotional intelligence. I first learned about the distinctions between givers and takers from Adam Grant's book *Give and Take*. Turns out, not only do people like takers less, but givers

are the most successful on average. Relationships are a two-way street. Don't be a taker.

3. **Not giving people a reason to respond.** The first message to a potential contact is critical. You're asking somebody to spend time—their most valuable, nonrenewable resource—responding to you. Remember, they don't know you or owe you. Getting a response requires you to be compelling, relevant, and interesting enough. I can't tell you how many times I've received a message from a stranger saying just "Hi" or "How are you?" without any additional context. The responsibility of the interaction falls on you, not the person you're messaging. If you're going to burden me with the effort of carrying a conversation that I didn't ask to start, you're trippin'. I can chit chat about how I am with my friends or my therapist. By being indirect and vague, you're placing a low value on my time and yours. Do the test with yourself: Would you respond to the message you're sending if you got it from a stranger?

4. **Taking it personally when people don't respond.** As humans, we're hardwired to think the world revolves around us. We create stories in our heads to try to make sense of why people do the things they do. The issue with that is you can't control how someone will respond to you and you'll never know anyone's intentions, so your stories are probably wrong. There are plenty of legitimate reasons why someone doesn't respond. Instead of assuming the worst, assume the best. Follow up politely, but don't let responses (or lack thereof) affect your mental state. If you need help with this, read *The Four Agreements* by Don Miguel Ruiz. Release your attachment to outcomes. Only you suffer if you don't.

5. **Not having a strategy for networking.** I get it, especially online, with so many options of people to connect with, it can be overwhelming to know where to start. Like anything else in life, if you don't have a strategy or process to succeed, you're aimless. Many people send messages out haphazardly and don't think about who they're targeting or why they're sending the note. That's like throwing a bunch of seeds on concrete and getting upset when they don't sprout. I'm not a gardener, but I'm pretty sure you're better off finding some quality soil and carefully planting and nurturing your plant babies. With a targeted strategy, you'll be able to get better results investing a fraction of the time.

6. **Thinking you can't network because you're an introvert.** All right, introverts, it's time to call you on your bullshit because I'm tired of your excuses! Networking is uncomfortable at some level to everyone. The whole point is getting out of your comfort zone. I get that it might not come as naturally to introverts, but relationship building is a skill, and like any skill, you can learn it. Gone are the days when you have to attend huge, live events to network. You know, you walk into an overcrowded conference hall, stand awkwardly near the snack table, talk to one guy named Peter about how bad the coffee is, and then pretend you're getting an important call so you can justify leaving early. The beautiful part of virtual networking is that it's perfectly suited for introverts. The internet, and especially LinkedIn, makes it really easy to qualify people prior to reaching out, communicate through written messages, and focus on one-to-one interaction rather than huge groups. Take advantage of this much less intimidating playground that's built for you to succeed.

7. **Feeling like you're bothering everyone.** Many people won't reach out because they don't want to be a bother. As long as you're not making mistake #2, you're probably not as annoying as you think. Bothering people also isn't the end of the world. If you pick the right types of people, show value, and come from a place of authenticity, you'll still bother some people; it's just part of the process. Are you going to let that scare you from going out and developing the amazing relationships that will ultimately help you live your dream life? I hope not. If someone doesn't want to respond to you, they won't. It's that simple. Also, recognize that some companies offer referral bonuses to employees when they refer candidates. Knowing that some people might have an incentive to pass you along can sometimes help reassure you.

8. **Not practicing.** How can you expect to be good at networking if you've never learned how to do it and you constantly avoid it? Networking is like a muscle: the less you do it, the more it atrophies. The best place to practice is in low-stakes, low-pressure environments. That's why, ideally, we build relationships when we don't need anything from them. That allows them to develop naturally and helps take away the perceived risk of interaction. I've included several exercises in this chapter to help you practice your relationship-building skills.

Now that you know what *not* to do, let's look at what to do instead.

Exercises: Networking

For downloadable digital versions of all the exercises referenced in this chapter, visit www.theremotejobcoach.com/book-resources.

Leverage Your Current Network

Often, when someone tells me they don't have any good contacts, they simply haven't taken the time to analyze and list all of the connections from their past. The first place to start is your current network, which is likely much more valuable than you realize.

EXERCISE: BUILDING YOUR NETWORK CONTACTS LIST

In his book *Do Over*, bestselling author Jon Acuff recommends the following exercise (which I've modified a bit) to take stock of your network. As you complete this exercise, brainstorm as many people as you can. By doing this once, you can use (and add to) this list for the rest of your life!

Who do I know that's smart about career issues?

Think of people you know who have done well in their careers, who have successfully made transitions, or who seem able to find new jobs and opportunities quickly or easily. They likely have wisdom, advice, and lessons they could share that would help you.

Who have I worked with?

Write down everyone you've worked with in the past several years. Focus on people you worked closely with, whose names you remember without having to look them up, and who will likely remember you.

Who do I know who is influential?

Do you know anyone who is notable in their industry (bonus points if it's the industry you're interested in)? Or who knows someone that is? Sometimes you won't have a direct contact into the industry or company you're interested in, but you know someone influential who can get you connected.

Who do I know that owns a business?

Even if someone owns a business that's unrelated to your career and job search, they can be a valuable contact, because, as Acuff points out, "business owners tend to know other business owners." They may know someone who is hiring for the kind of position you're looking for.

Who do I follow online who is in my desired career space?

List all of the people you follow online who are currently doing what you want to be doing. With intentional effort, you might be able to build a relationship with those people, and who knows, maybe you could end up with valuable career advice or even a job opportunity.

Who are the connectors in my network?

This last category is my addition to Acuff's framework. In his book *The Tipping Point*, Malcolm Gladwell talks about connectors. These are people who have a special gift for building relationships. They always seem to be in the center of social circles, introducing people to each other, and they occupy many different worlds. Think about the communities you exist in and the people who tend to be the glue in those communities. Those connectors can be powerful allies in your job search.

Now, review your list. Chances are, you have brainstormed way more names than you thought you would. With this information, you can strategize how to get in touch with these people again to tell them about your job search and ask for help. There will be different levels of familiarity and ways of speaking with these people. For those you know well who will support you no matter what, you can send them a message about your job search and ask them for any leads on jobs or introductions to people in companies. For people who are acquaintances, I recommend warming up the conversation a bit before asking for anything.

Pro Tip: Leverage Your Weak Ties

Every network has strong and weak ties. Your strong ties are your first connections—the people you have a direct relationship with. Your weak ties are your second, third, and so on connections. You don't know these people directly, but you know people who know them—essentially, friends of friends.

It can feel more comfortable to reach out to your strong ties, but in networking, everything you could ever need is in your weak ties. Once you get one, two, or three contacts outside your immediate network, it opens up the entire world to you. There's even a running theory about us all being six connections away from Kevin Bacon, a famous American actor. When you expand your efforts to your weak ties, you can discover that with the right connections, people are much more accessible than you might've initially believed.

THE STRENGTH OF WEAK TIES

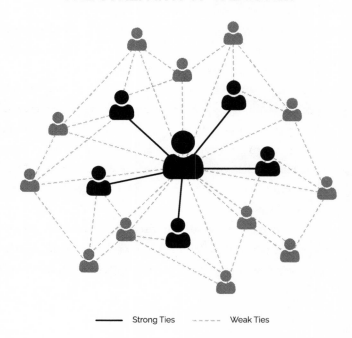

——— Strong Ties   ~ ~ ~ ~ Weak Ties

Expand Your Network

When you're building relationships, you don't have enough energy or time to target everyone. The benefit of online networking is being able to prequalify the relevance of a potential connection prior to reaching out.

On the internet (and LinkedIn specifically), you can use a far more targeted strategy. Because people are encouraged to put their current role, job history, and even personal information on their profiles, it gives us the opportunity to build relationships on a deeper level without wasting time on the wrong people. If you haven't used LinkedIn much, you'll be surprised at how engaging it can be, and how willing people are to connect.

Your advantage? Well, most people are bad at this. By just being better than most people at making friends online, you'll immediately stand out. And you're reading this book, so you will be.

EXERCISE: TARGET PERSONAS

First and foremost, understand the most effective types of people to proactively target:

- **People who do what you want to do**: They already have the role, work on the team, or work within the company you're interested in. They can provide helpful insider knowledge through an informational interview, and if you end up applying to a position at their company, they are a connection point and might even act as a sponsor for you internally.

- **People who hire people who do what you do**: These are decision makers or stakeholders in getting you hired. They could be hiring managers, recruiters, or other people who have a direct influence on hiring decisions.

- **Indirect mentors:** These are people from a different industry, type of role, or company who can support your job search efforts and potentially provide connections or advice.

By targeting these individuals, you'll get more bang for your buck in your networking efforts.

NETWORKING TARGET PERSONA

SOCIAL CAPITAL

RELEVANCE

Indirect Mentors

Low Relevance
High Social Capital

Direct Mentors

High Relevance
High Social Capital

Irrelevant Connections

Low Relevance
Low Social Capital

Potential Mentees

High Relevance
Low Social Capital

Create Digital Proximity with the 3 Cs

We've got the "who," so now let's talk about the "how" of making connections. The first step is to create *digital proximity*, which we talked about previously. The idea is to create a digital closeness, so when you message someone, they are familiar enough with you that they'll likely respond. Put yourself in the same sphere as your target personas and establish some kind of common ground, and the first connection will be easier to make.

The best way to create digital proximity to your target personas is through the 3 Cs:

- **Current network:** Start consistently connecting with people in your current network who fall into one of the three target categories or who may be able to get you connected to such people. This is the easiest way to start networking because there's already familiarity. Reach out to former coworkers, high school classmates, clubs you used to be a part of, and anyone on the lists you made in the Network Contact List exercise.

- **Communities:** After you establish your target personas, think about where they spend their time and attention online and get involved in relevant communities. When targeting a specific company, find out where online they do events or get people together— webinars, virtual conferences, user group Q&As, and so on. Become a customer if you can. Remote-specific communities on social media, like Facebook and LinkedIn groups, can also be helpful to expand your network. Focus on connecting with anyone who posts a lot as well as the group admins, as they can be gatekeepers to opportunities.

- **Content:** Wherever your targeted company or potential connections post online, make sure you're part of the conversation.

Commenting and engaging on social posts becomes one of the easiest and highest impact ways to create digital proximity, and you can even filter on LinkedIn to show all the content posted by employees at your target organizations in one view.

By interacting with your target personas in these ways, you establish subconscious familiarity. When you send a connection request (being sure to always add a note), it's not the first time they've seen your name pop up in their feed—which makes a huge difference.

Lead with Value

After creating digital proximity, start connecting directly, keeping one big question in mind: *Are you creating more or less work for the people you're communicating with?*

If chatting with you makes someone's life harder, they aren't incentivized to do it. It's that simple. Especially if they don't know you, it's your responsibility to create a bridge of trust with them before making an ask (e.g., to look at your résumé, sponsor you to a hiring manager, or help you get a job). Have you ever been approached by a stranger who's effectively demanding your time or energy? You hate it, right? Well, the same goes for the random people you've asked to review your application. Be aware of your first impressions and the weight they carry.

Instead, make interacting with you easy, and add value to their life however possible. Focus first on what you can give before trying to get something. In addition, when you reach out, it's your responsibility to lead and give people enough information to have a compelling conversation. A lot of times people don't respond because the person messaging them is boring and irrelevant. Be creative here, while understanding that value can be provided by anyone in three ways:

1. **Ideas**: What unique ideas do you have about their company, role, or industry that could be helpful? (Constructive feedback, thoughtful insights, task assistance)

2. **Information**: What relevant information can you find to pass along that's salient? (Articles, industry trends, upcoming events)

3. **Introductions**: How can you facilitate a mutually beneficial relationship for another two humans that should know each other? (Clients, partners, job candidates)

I get it, it's not always easy to know what to offer. And some of us are more senior than others, with bigger networks or more experience to leverage for value. Fortunately, providing value doesn't need to be a complicated, time-consuming thing. My friend and career coach Madeline Mann argues for "60 seconds of value," using five techniques to add value in a small window of time: (1) make an intro, (2) share resources, (3) invite to communities, (4) brainstorm ideas, and (5) engage on social media.

EXERCISE: YOUR NETWORKING VALUE

If you're still struggling to find ways to provide value to someone, do some research to spark ideas:

1. Look at their content and activity on LinkedIn. If they post consistently, you can make some assumptions that they are open to engaging. Value is subjective—to many, likes and comments are valuable. Everyone who posts is vain enough to want engagement. No one wants crickets.

2. Search their name on Google to discover their website, other social media profiles, and more context for what they will find valuable.

3. See what groups they are a part of, including volunteering, and what they care about. The communities someone occupies tell you a lot about what they value.

4. See what you can find out about their personal life (within reason… I'm not advocating for stalking!).

5. Look up their education (where they went to school, certifications they have, courses they've taken that are relevant to you, and so on).

Then, based on this information, ask yourself: *What would help them in their job (or interests) that they could be missing?*

Change the Input: Reframe Your Mindset

Every communication is a micro sale to the next step.

So many people go for the home run in one message. If your first message to someone is you're interested in a job and you'd like them to look at your résumé, you've ruined your first impression. Unless you have a direct, warm tie to that person, you haven't earned the right to do that. It's like asking someone to marry you before you've asked them on a date!

Think about the job search process as a series of small steps where you're selling the immediate next piece of communication. For example, when you're sending in an application, the goal isn't to get the job, the goal is to get a response. Once you get a response, the goal is to get an interview. Once you get an interview, it's to get

> a callback. And so on and so forth. If you look at it from the granular, step-by-step level, you won't get lost in the macro picture, where it's easy to get ahead of yourself. When you get too far ahead of yourself, it creates more attachment to the overall outcome and doesn't allow you to appreciate progress.

Build Trust

Relationships aren't transactions. It's best to intentionally build your network before you desperately need a job, because you can come from a place of not needing anything. The more trust you build, the more confident you can feel making direct asks.

If somebody ends up sponsoring your résumé or referring you to a job, it's a *huge* opportunity. With opportunity comes responsibility, and them putting their reputation on the line is a sign of trust. Be sure to thank them, and don't drop the relationship just because you got what you wanted. Building and maintaining trust is a continual process, and it can be lost much quicker than gained.

Resource: Informational Interview Guide

While networking and meeting connections at your target roles or companies, consider asking for an informational interview. It's one of the best ways to get insight into a job role, a company, or an industry.

Informational interviews have many benefits:

- Get firsthand, relevant information about the realities of working within a particular field, industry, or position. This kind of information is not always available online.

- Find out about career paths you didn't know existed.

- Get tips and insider knowledge about how to prepare for and land your first career position.

- Learn what it's like to work at a specific organization.

- Initiate a professional relationship and expand your network of contacts in a specific career field; meet people who may forward job leads to you in the future.

- Stand out during the job application process.

Informational interviews are commonplace in job searching, but there are nuances to ensure you are effective and respectful in getting the information you need to progress your remote job search. Visit www.theremotejobcoach.com/book-resources for a guide on informational interviews, with tips on who to target, how to make the ask, and how to conduct the interview itself.

Networking Routines

We've covered the intention and value portions of the networking equation, so now let's talk consistency. Remember: the biggest mistake you can make is neglecting your network until you need something. Make networking a habit, and you won't have to think about it; you'll just do it, and it will always be there to support you.

DAILY ROUTINE: THE 5X5X5 METHOD

Networking success is not easily quantifiable, and the success criteria that do exist—like getting a job or other opportunity—are outside of our control. The most effective relationship-building output is consistent, yet manageable. With this 5x5x5 method, you have new metrics of success beyond getting a job. You can spend a small amount of effort each day, with targeted and intentional structure, and compound the effects over time. While this exercise is written with LinkedIn in mind, you can adapt it to any social media platform.

Find a time during the day when you can segment about fifteen to thirty minutes of focused energy. (In the beginning, this exercise will likely take closer to thirty minutes, but with practice, it will go more quickly.) Make it the same time every day and block it in your calendar. The goal is consistency, not perfection.

First 5: Leave 5 Thoughtful Comments

The first step is to leave five thoughtful comments. Visit the profiles of target companies, relevant groups, target personas, or strong people in your network. Find a recent post and leave a thoughtful comment. For ease, bookmark your favorite creators or those you want to engage with on a frequent basis. At the time of this writing LinkedIn also has a notification bell feature that will let you know when someone posts.

In your comments, focus on relevance and intention. Your goal is to show off your expertise and be part of the conversation. Remember others can see your comments (as well as your headline and photo next to your comment), so make them insightful. Comments are pieces of original micro-content. Especially for those who don't want to create their own full posts, commenting is a nice, low-effort way to find your voice and create an online presence while simultaneously building targeted relationships.

Don't know what to say? Here's a formula for writing the perfect comment:

(Compliment) + (Your Perspective) + (Open-Ended Question)

Second 5: Connect with 5 Targeted People

Next, make five new targeted connections. You can use many different strategies:

- Add people from relevant groups and communities you've joined, and start up a conversation based on the mutual group.

- Search hashtags and add people talking about [keyword].

- Comment on interesting and relevant articles and posts, then add the person who posted the content, and "Add Note."

- Add those working at companies you're interested in.

- Add those doing the job you want to be doing, or those in a position to hire for that job.

- Add people who went to the same school or have a similar background.

Third 5: Unfollow 5 Irrelevant People

Finally, you're going to select five people to unfollow. This one is counterintuitive for most people. Your feed is a direct reflection of your past decisions. By taking out less relevant "fluff" from your timeline, you can more easily see the good stuff. We train the algorithms. You can either train them to serve the side of you that likes thirst trapping Instagram models, pimple popping, or puppies—or you can train it to show you more applicable and pertinent content, which will improve your mental health as well as your job search. Go with your gut and your intuition about who to unfollow. And don't worry about accidentally eliminating a network contact that could later be useful. By unfollowing, you'll still be connected to them on LinkedIn—you just won't see their posts in your feed.

With this 5×5×5 approach, you will achieve several important goals:

- You're no longer a stranger to your target personas because you're creating subconscious familiarity through engagement.

- You create an "in" for the DMs—when someone recognizes your name from their notifications, they're more likely to open and respond to your direct message.

- You show off your expertise by leaving insightful comments.

- You get in the habit of networking and cleaning your feed.

- You expand your ability to see other profiles and gain more weak ties.

Day after day, as you get in the flow, you can get each 5 down to five to ten minutes of effort. If you don't think you have time to do this a few times a week for the rest of your life, I'd challenge you to show me your phone statistics to see how much you spend on social media already. Most people don't realize how many hours they consume absolute garbage on Facebook, Instagram, YouTube, TikTok, and all these other sites. Convert thirty minutes of mindless scrolling to intentional engagement and watch your life change forever!

WEEKLY ROUTINE: BOTTOM OF THE THREAD

Now that we have a daily networking routine, let's add a weekly routine to re-engage with people we've lost touch with. I'll start with the assumption that most of us don't delete our message threads, whether from:

1. Texts

2. WhatsApp

3. Facebook Messenger

4. Instagram DMs

5. LinkedIn

6. Email

Over time, these threads take up space in our various inboxes. Conversations get buried in a slew of other messages, and we lose touch with people we truly value for no other reason than life getting in the way. There's no need to blame either party. In the age of information overload, it's impossible for us to stay up with all of our notifications, emails, messages, and so on. But networking is as much about maintaining your current relationships as it is about creating new ones. The tendency for messages to collect in our inbox provides us with an interesting opportunity, which I originally learned from my friend Eduardo Lopez and since coined as the "Bottom of the Thread" exercise.

Each week, set aside time on your calendar to scroll down to the bottom of your messages on one of the platforms you use. As you descend, you'll start to see old communications you forgot existed, which may be frightening. If you can stomach wading through regrettable drunk texts to your ex, you might also find some threads with contacts you wish you had stayed in contact with.

Pick up to three people to send a message to, with the intention of getting back in touch. Don't open with an ask or favor regarding your job search. Instead opt for a simple: "Hey XXX, it's been a while! I was thinking of you and wondering what's changed since we last spoke. Would love to catch up soon."

If these people feel the same way about you, they'll be thrilled you're putting in the effort to keep in touch. As you do this more and more, you may find out something about someone's job situation or life that can become a gateway to your next opportunity. Hint: always be looking to help provide them with opportunities too! Remember: intros, ideas, and information. When you keep your ears open for others, you're more valuable as a result.

QUARTERLY ROUTINE: NETWORK CATCH-UP CALLS

After reengaging with old contacts and creating new ones on a daily basis, your network will be taking a nice shape. This is an exciting phenomenon, and I recommend you ride the wave of momentum like you're riding a gravy train on biscuit wheels.

To best do that, make catching up with those who are most important to you a nonnegotiable. I have a number of close contacts in my life who I want to make sure I don't lose touch with. You likely have some as well. Ask them if they'd be interested in setting up quarterly catch-up calls, and take the lead to set up a calendar invite if they give you the thumbs-up.

Once you've done that, you don't have the excuse of falling out of touch, because at minimum, you'll have four catch-up points per year on the books. Of course, life changes and people need to reschedule or cancel from time to time, but this strategy is to keep people top of mind. Just by having the calls on the calendar, you may find yourself more enticed to communicate in between discussions, and then you won't have to be searching the bottom of the thread to find them anymore.

Always Be Connecting

By intentionally building my network, I've met so many people that have benefited my life, never knowing that they would be as important to me as they've become. Beyond a job search, from a personal perspective, many valuable relationships develop because you know someone who knows someone. You could even meet your future spouse or your new best friend.

As you cultivate and care for your network on a regular basis, growing existing relationships while planting the seeds for new ones, you can start reaping the benefits as you go. By consistently implementing these networking techniques, you'll be as unstoppable as Joey Chestnut at a hot dog eating contest.

CHAPTER 8

CHANGE THE CHANNEL

Optionality Through Freelance Work

WHEN I MET WESTON IN JULY OF 2020, HE WAS WORKING TWELVE-hour shifts in a Tesla factory. We jumped on a phone call to talk about remote job coaching. During that first conversation, it was apparent he wanted change, but it was likely going to be a long way until he got there. As he described it, he felt trapped in a cage, stuck due to a common catch-22: "You can't get a job without experience, but you need the job to get experience." He worked hard, but he just didn't have the skills or experience yet to make the full transition to remote work.

He was a great fit for my eight-week accelerator program ($2,500 at the time), but he'd just paid his taxes and rent. Since he was working a low wage factory job assembling cars, the drain from his recent expenditures meant he only had $40 in his bank account. That's when the unthinkable happened, which was something I'd never experienced before as a coach.

He asked to put a $20 down payment on the $2,500 program. I watched him do the mental math as he outlined a cohesive strategy for how he'd pay me over the course of 2 months by taking extra shifts and earning overtime. I was stunned. Never before had a potential client demonstrated this level of commitment.

Here he was, putting up 50% of what he had to join my program. I could see in his eyes he was going to make this happen and I'd never felt more confident about a client's potential. Either that, or I'd be taking a massive risk and receive only 0.8% of a complete payment and learn a valuable lesson myself.

I onboarded him with $20 in hand and a payment plan in place. Throughout the program, Weston would literally listen to the video lessons of my course on his headphones at work while assembling cars. During his breaks, he would go on the LinkedIn mobile app, engage with posts, and send networking messages. He spent his nights and weekends taking courses to upskill his SEO chops. He absorbed everything he learned and took action right away.

By the end of the program, I knew he was special, and I hired him part-time to freelance for me as a marketing assistant. I introduced him to other business owners in my network and he landed enough clients to quit his job. At the time of writing this, over two years later, he manages part of my team as a freelancer and has helped tremendously in the efforts to bring this book to life. He loves the freelance lifestyle because of the opportunity to work with different organizations on a variety of interesting projects, the freedom to set his own schedule, and the flexibility to travel.

No more assembly lines for Weston. And it was all due to one decision and commitment to himself to change his life. He boasts a full roster of freelance clients and fully supports himself as an SEO specialist. Freelancing was Weston's path to remote work.

As a freelancer, you can prioritize variety—an assortment of projects, clients, and even skills you're able to monetize to support your remote lifestyle. Having a litany of clients, just like having a litany of channels to select, gives you an abundance of options to flip through.

Monetize Your Skills with Freelance Work

Freelancing is a great bridge for many people joining the remote workforce, and it can be a smart choice for those who want greater flexibility or who are interested in making additional income on the side. It's not necessarily easy, but there's a low barrier to entry because you don't need any formal education to get started. All you need is a marketable skill to offer, which you can build with Google, YouTube, and a solid work ethic.

The definition of a freelancer according to Investopedia is "an individual who earns money on a per-job or per-task basis, usually for short-term work." A freelancer might have a variety of projects and companies they work for at once until the projects are complete, or they may even work long-term with companies, just on a contract model as opposed to being a full-time employee with benefits.

According to Upwork (a freelance marketplace platform), as of 2022, fifty-eight million people freelance in the United States, and it is destined to become the work style for the majority of the US workforce by 2027. The industry contributes over $1 trillion to the US economy every year, and even companies like Google hire more freelancers than permanent employees as of writing this.

There are many reasons this trend will continue on both the employee and company sides.

Freelancers
- Those with in-demand skills can charge high fees while maintaining more autonomy over their schedule and the decisions they make on a day-to-day basis.

- They can work on a variety of different and interesting projects instead of being locked into one organization.

- They can start with just the knowledge they already have with very low to no costs.

Employers
- They can hire on a project basis and mitigate long-term risk of hiring full-time employees.

- In countries where they can't hire full-time employees because of tax or regulatory implications, they can hire freelancers for contract work.

- It offers the business more flexibility without needing to offer certain benefits for each of their contracts.

Since freelancers get to choose how they do their work, then in most cases, as long as it's logistically feasible, they may choose to work remotely. With this kind of flexibility, it's no surprise that remote freelancing jobs come in a wide variety. According to CareerSidekick, these are the top ten highest paying freelance jobs of 2022:

1. Copywriting

2. Software engineer/web developer

3. Digital marketing consultant

4. Social media manager

5. SEO specialist

6. Media buyer

7. Photographer/videographer

8. Web designer

9. Data analyst

10. Sales/lead generation specialist

I imagine over the years, this list will change as other skills and new jobs become more lucrative. But the point is, as long as you have a marketable hard skill that can be done remotely, freelancing might be a good path for you.

Change the Input: Reframe Your Mindset

You don't need to do it all by yourself.

Most people think of freelancing as a solo profession, but delegating is a huge part of what differentiates freelancers who are stuck from those who grow.

Alexandra Fasulo, also known as The Freelance Fairy, started as a freelance writer and wrote blogs for her clients completely alone for the first five years. By that time, she knew what her clients wanted and expected. So, she started building systems, and ultimately a freelance agency to help deliver in a more scalable way. As she explained in an Instagram post, when clients now place an order for a blog, her team of writers does the writing, her agency manager delivers the order, and she's taken herself out of the process.

When you're first starting out, doing hands-on work is beneficial. It gets you experience with the processes that work and keeps you close to client feedback so you can iterate on your standard operating procedures. But at some point, you'll want to consider what parts of the work you can outsource. Start small and start with a task you know how to do but either don't want to, isn't within your expertise, or isn't as profitable for you to do. Hire other freelancers to help you freelance!

Is Freelancing Right for You?

There are several reasons that freelancing might be right for you:

- **Expertise:** Maybe you've got specific expertise in a particular area that is often done as project-based work rather than a full-time position—for example: graphic designer, writer, web designer, and so on.

- **Flexibility and Autonomy:** Perhaps you want the flexibility to work with different types of people and projects, or maybe you want the option of choosing your own work hours, or how you do your work.

- **Diversification:** You want to diversify your income sources among various types of opportunities. Freelancing is a good way to earn extra money without putting all your eggs in one basket.

- **Gap filler:** If you're between jobs, freelancing can be used to prevent gaps in your résumé. There's a flow that comes with being employed or having projects you're contributing to. Freelance work can help you keep your skills sharp.

- **Transition:** Especially if you're transitioning into a different industry, job role, or specialty, you may lack the experience to get a full-time position. Freelancing can beef up your résumé in that industry or role, and expose you to different types of organizations and work styles to help you transition.

The Challenges of Freelancing

While freelancing comes with many benefits, it also comes with unique challenges.

- **The race to the lowest number:** Many freelancers compete based on lowering their rates, and because talent is located all over the world, a low rate in the US can be a high rate in a place like the Philippines. This means the quality of talent a business can find for less money is always a consideration. If you could have the same task completed at about the same quality for ten dollars or fifty dollars, which would you choose? Eventually, if you're competing on price with someone whose cost of living is a fraction of your own, you'll be unable to sustain yourself. There's always going to be someone willing to charge less than you, so find ways to stand out and prove your value and unique differentiation so you're not competing on price every time.

- **Unpredictability:** Some freelancers secure stable, long-term, full-time employment with companies as independent contractors, but for many freelancers, work is often feast or famine. You might be overwhelmed with work one month and struggle to find any paying gigs the next. Not knowing when you'll get your next paycheck can lead to stress, debt, and sleepless nights.

- **Finding clients and getting paid:** As a freelancer, it's not enough to be a writer, programmer, designer, or whatever. You also have to be a salesperson. You're responsible not only for securing clients but also making sure they actually pay you, which for some people can be as much fun as drinking a garlic milkshake.

- **Lack of benefits:** Freelancers don't get any of the extra perks that employees do—health insurance, sick days, vacation time, matching 401(k) contributions, stock options, and so on.

- **Hidden costs:** If an employee and a freelancer are paid the same amount, the freelancer is probably making less money. This is because there are extra costs associated with freelancing that need to be factored in. As an employee, your company usually covers part of your healthcare, and may even help with stipends for everything you need to complete your job— computer, software, office chair, and so on. As a freelancer, you're responsible for all those things. You're also paid for the hours or for the job, as opposed to a salary. When factoring in all your non-billable time—hours spent finding clients, working on professional development, completing administrative tasks, and so on, you'll see there are a lot of costs involved that eat into a freelancer's profits.

- **Isolation:** I talked previously about how remote work can be lonely. This goes twofold for freelancers. As a freelancer, you're usually on your own, without coworkers or a boss. For the introverted hermits out there, that might sound like a dream. But it also means you don't have anyone on your team to give you advice, mentor you, or just have a chat about how your day is going.

- **The logistics of owning a business:** If you're a freelancer, you effectively own your own business, which comes with a lot of work—often frustrating and confusing minutiae. You have to think about taxes, legal liability, and more.

For some people, these difficulties are deal breakers, which is fine. The most important part of this process is knowing yourself and what you're willing to trade off. By being aware of and preparing for these challenges, you can make the best educated decision for yourself.

Finding Gigs

When you're looking for freelance gigs, you're not trying to land *one* job, but multiple jobs, so it's more effective to pursue several opportunities at once. One of the biggest challenges of freelancing is just finding your first one. My friend David Gauthier, the Freelance Business Coach, outlines these steps to help you get over that initial hurdle.

1. Learn a skill, preferably a high-value one, and one you see yourself becoming an expert in for the long term. Focus on that *one* skill. A lot of people try to learn and offer too many services at once. Being a generalist holds them back from reaching their true potential with the one skill they could master.

2. Get good enough at said skill to offer it as a service. A good way to determine this is to ask yourself, "Would I pay for my services?" You can also get feedback from people in your network—coworkers, social media connections, friends, etc.

3. Create an "MVP"—minimum viable product.

    a. At this phase, you can create your own projects and "hire yourself." Let's say you're an email copywriter; you could write an email sequence and throw it up in a Google Doc.

b. Share the work you did for yourself as a case study and offer to do the same for people in your network for free in exchange for testimonials. The freelance marketplaces are highly competitive. Especially when you're just starting out, you'll be much more likely to land your first gigs by helping friends. That's exactly how Weston was able to build experience and get out of his catch-22.

4. At this stage, you've got three to five solid work samples. It's time to start putting yourself out there and charging. David recommends picking one freelance marketplace and one social media platform to start—for example, Upwork and LinkedIn. Marketplaces get a bad rap for their fierce competition and the idea that in order to win, you need to be the cheapest. There's some truth to that, but these sites are also filled with thousands of warm prospects ready to buy. Platforms like Upwork and Fiverr are a great way to kick off your freelance business, and they're the main income source for a lot of freelancers.

    a. Optimize your profiles and treat them as funnels for your business. David compares freelance marketplaces to Amazon. The freelancer is the product, and the buyer is the client. You need to find ways to be unique and sell yourself. Having good reviews from past clients is critical—it pushes you higher in the search algorithm and builds trust with potential new clients by providing social proof of your skills. An easy way to get early reviews is to do work for friends and have them hire you through the platform.

    b. Send *custom* messages and proposals/cover letters. The tips in the next chapter about applying (particularly the section on value assets) can be useful. However, be conscious about how much time you spend on a proposal. Your effort should be proportional to the potential payoff. You want a good return on investment for your time and energy.

c.   Be active in the community you serve.

d.   Do this until you get a client. Repeat each step until you do.

Ideally, you can reach a point as a freelancer where you set up your profile or a website and clients come to you. Until then, be ready to put in the legwork to get your first gigs.

Resource: Gig and Freelance Work

For a list of websites to find gig and freelance work, visit www.theremotejobcoach.com/book-resources.

Opening Doors of Opportunity: The True Beauty of Freelance Work

My greater purpose in life is helping those for whom remote work can be the biggest lifesaver: underprivileged populations, those with disabilities, and refugees. So to me, the best part of freelance work is the opportunities it offers to groups often left out of traditional work environments.

Fahim Ul Karim is a great example of the power of remote freelancing. Fahim was a freelance graphic designer from Bangladesh featured in a short video from Running Remote (which you can find on YouTube; just search "Running Remote Fahim."). Fahim had Duchenne Muscular Dystrophy (DMD), a genetic disorder leading to progressive muscle degeneration and weakness. As a result of his physical disability, he had to leave school in Grade 8. Eventually he learned about the possibility of earning money online. In 2016, using money his mother saved selling hand-sewn quilts, he bought a laptop. After spending three months learning graphic design from a DVD, he opened a Fiverr account and received his first job the very next day. He continued working as a freelancer through platforms like Fiverr and Upwork, becoming a respected designer with high customer satisfaction. He earned enough money to buy land and build a house for his family, and during the COVID-19 pandemic, he became his family's sole breadwinner. Sadly, he passed away in November 2020.

In the video from Running Remote, Fahim refers to "the curse of unemployment." Many of us in more privileged positions take work for granted. We complain about it far more than we value it, but for many others, being able to work—to contribute to the workforce in a dignified way—is life-changing. It's a blessing that isn't afforded to all people equally, but remote work, particularly freelancing, offers new opportunities that have never been around before. Many organizations have recognized the potential for remote work to change lives and are doing great work in this space. Organizations like Na'amal, Jobs for Humanity, MIT React, Nomad Skillshare, and Techfugees, all of which I've done volunteer work with, help underprivileged talent upskill so they can work remotely. This is the true beauty of remote work and what it can bring to our society.

Freelancing: Flexibility for All

The biggest benefit and challenge of freelancing is the same: flexibility. As a freelancer, you have more control over what, how, and when you work. But this opportunity also can be seen as a challenge if you're not ready for the responsibility of owning your own business, dealing with taxes, and finding clients. Knowing yourself and what situation makes the most sense for you is critical in determining whether freelancing is an option you want to choose.

CHAPTER 9

PRESS ENTER

The Application Process That Puts You in the Game

WHILE I WAS WORKING WITH DONALDO, HE FOUND A POSITION WITH an email marketing company that was 100% remote and hired employees globally. That was one of his top priorities since he was from Honduras. There was a problem, though: the listing was set to expire that same night.

We devised a plan for him to do something creative, all while being efficient with time. The listing was for a product management role, which requires you to be somewhat technical and know your way around the company's software. In this case, one of the key features of this company's platform was their landing page builder.

So, Donaldo registered a free account on their site so he could get his hands on the software and become more familiar with its functionality. He loaded the landing page builder and took some time to mess around with it. A few YouTube videos later and he had the grasp he needed.

He created a short video, about a minute and a half, of him explaining his credentials and why he was a good fit for the position, using the job description as a guide. He coded the video into the landing page, customized a résumé and cover letter, and then completed the application. Not only that, but he sent this custom landing page directly to the hiring manager via email and LinkedIn before the application closed that night. Among a slew of cookie-cutter applications, Donaldo stood out. Within the next few days he was invited to interview for the job because of his creativity in the application process.

Most job seekers pay absolutely zero attention to strategy when they apply. It's as if they're smashing all the buttons on the remote at once, hoping that one of them will get them to the program they're looking for. To enter yourself into a company's purview, it's far more effective to take a thoughtful and focused approach, pressing the right button for the job.

Common Application Mistakes

Before you even start sending out applications, let's go over what *not* to do, so you can immediately separate yourself from others. (Some of this information is referenced in the Doist article "The 8 Biggest Mistakes to Avoid When Applying For a Remote Job" by Andrew Gobran.) Committing these errors is normal. I have, and a majority of other job seekers have too. Don't beat yourself up about it; use this as an opportunity to improve.

MISTAKE #1: OVER-QUALIFYING OR UNDER-QUALIFYING YOURSELF

Be realistic when evaluating your candidacy for a job. Over-qualifying yourself is one of the easiest ways to immediately end up in the application black hole. If you've held mostly entry-level jobs, don't mistake yourself as qualified for a leadership position at a new company. And if you're switching industries or lack experience in the type of role you're applying for, don't fall into the trap of thinking you're above doing something more entry-level. Oftentimes, in a remote, distributed team environment, the important thing is to start *somewhere*, especially if you've never worked in that particular industry. That may mean feeling like you're taking a demotion, but it doesn't have to be something to look at negatively.

Remember, your goal is to optimize your lifestyle here. If a job allows you to live the life you want to live, it's a promotion—a step closer to your goals and desired future. Also remember the path isn't always a straight line. The job you take now isn't the job you're committing to forever.

This doesn't mean you need to check off every item on a job listing's requirements, either. Under-qualifying yourself is also a mistake. Most people think they need to have *all* the qualifications in a job posting when you really only need 70 to 80%. Don't sell yourself short, but be open to trade-offs.

MISTAKE #2: OVEREMPHASIZING REMOTE WORK

Stop telling companies you want to work for them specifically because you're desperate to work remotely. While that may be true, it's a red flag for the employer. It's like telling someone you only want to date them because they're rich. Companies don't want to be your sugar daddy or momma.

Plus, for your own sake, being remote shouldn't be the *only* reason you want to work for a company. Being remote isn't enough to sustain your motivation and satisfaction with a job over the long term. Try to find other reasons to get on board with their mission, culture, and the role itself. The more you can align what you can provide with what a company provides, the better.

MISTAKE #3: QUANTITY OVER QUALITY

Getting a remote job isn't a numbers game. The amount of applications you submit doesn't matter; what matters is how many quality job *offers* you receive. What's more, as the volume of applications you complete increases, the level of qualification and attention you can give each one decreases.

If you're applying to dozens and dozens of jobs, it's likely that many of them aren't the best fit, and you won't be able to establish a deep relationship with the company because you'll be focusing on the next application already. At that point it's also easy to lose track of where you've applied, what part of the process you're in with what company, and who you should follow up with. It becomes a shit show. It's akin to going on a dating app looking for love but blindfolding yourself and swiping back and forth rapidly.

If your target is everything, you'll hit nothing. It's far more effective to customize your applications. Part of the process I outline in this chapter is going to be unscalable, and for a good reason: the point is to improve your chances of being hired at one of your target companies for a role you're qualified for, not just anywhere for a random job.

MISTAKE #4: NOT DOING YOUR RESEARCH

It's incredible how many people are willing to send out a résumé or get on the phone with a recruiter without an understanding of what a company does. How can you prove you're able to provide value to an organization if you don't even know what they do? And if you can't prove your value, why would they hire you?

Once you get away from the knee-jerk reaction of applying to everything that looks somewhat relevant, you can redirect that energy into research of the companies you're actually interested in. And this research doesn't have to be time intensive. Since very few job seekers do their due diligence when applying, spending twenty minutes browsing through the company website can make you look like Sherlock Holmes in comparison.

MISTAKE #5: NO PERSONALIZED COVER LETTER

Sending a customized cover letter is a great way of showing a company you're serious while also helping you stand out in the process. Even if a cover letter is not "required," create one! Between you and another candidate of equal skill and stature, a cover letter can be the way to separate yourself.

It will also help you articulate your value in relation to the job and company, further explain a career transition, and provide additional context that's not in your résumé. Some recruiters and hiring managers have grown to dislike cover letters. Why? Because most candidates copy and paste the same cover letter for every job and just switch the company name. That won't be you. Later in the book I'll discuss what makes an attention-worthy cover letter and provide you with a template you can steal from me. Note: the only time I would advise not sending a cover letter is if it explicitly says not to.

MISTAKE #6: NO ONLINE REPUTATION

We're in an age where your online reputation is as real as your offline reputation. If a company is interested in your candidacy, they will search for you on Google, LinkedIn, or other social media. What will they find?

It's your responsibility to be intentional about your online persona, and if they don't find anything at all about you, you're losing an opportunity to paint the narrative of your expertise. If you come out from hiding, you'll be surprised with how many opportunities become available to you, and the difference it makes in your ability to build relationships.

MISTAKE #7: DOING THE BARE MINIMUM

I've heard Boomers tell stories about walking into a business, giving the owner a firm handshake while looking them in the eye, and being offered a job on the spot because they know how to use a broom.

Finding a job doesn't work that way anymore, and sending in an application just to twiddle your thumbs while you wait for a reply won't cut it either. The top remote companies receive an exorbitant amount of applications, and it's required to go above and beyond to get noticed.

Change the Input: Reframe Your Mindset

Your job search is not about you—
it's about the benefit to the company.

It's easy to get self-centered in a job search. When you want a new job, the universe seems to revolve around you. You may find yourself taking things more personally, especially when receiving a rejection or no replies at all from your efforts. But the reality is, no one *really* cares that you need a job. At least, there's no way they can care more than you.

When approaching a job search, be as empathetic as possible to recruiters, hiring managers, and decision makers. Their job is to hire the right candidate for their team. They're going to act in their own personal self-interest, what they think is right for the company, and in line with whatever incentives they have.

You represent a risk. Think of it like this: if someone hires the wrong person, they can potentially lose their job. Not only that, but they likely have a range of other responsibilities other than hiring for this position that they're juggling behind the scenes. When you take a step back and observe the situation for what it is without the emotion and attachment of your needs, you can more easily distinguish the objective reality that not everything is about you.

With that perspective, you can instead focus on the problem you're solving for the company and for that person. Get yourself in the employer's head and think about how you can mitigate their risk, gain their trust, and show them exactly how you're going to help them. As much as possible, take yourself, the way you speak, and the way you think out of the equation. Think about the company's point of view and how you can be an asset for them, and articulate that value in language consistent with theirs. Be you, but be you in the context of being a solution to the company's problem.

The Unique Application Sequence: A Solution to the Black Hole of Rejected Résumés

A remote job listing can easily get hundreds of applications. Only a handful of those applicants will be chosen for interviews, and the remainder will be shot into the black hole of rejected résumés, never to see the light again. If you've spent much time applying for jobs, especially if you've made any of the common application mistakes listed before, you've probably been the victim of this black hole. It's one of the most frustrating and demoralizing experiences of the job search.

Part of the struggle for many job seekers is going up against an applicant tracking system (ATS) when they apply. An ATS, according to Jobscan, is a human resources software that acts as a database for job applicants. It helps them organize, search, and communicate with large groups of applicants. Not to mention, 99% of Fortune 500 companies use these systems as part of their recruitment strategy.

Because the ATS is parsing data from the résumés, it helps recruiters and hiring managers score and rank candidates based on their potential match with the job description. And while there are some recruiters who do glance at all résumés that come through, there are situations where it's just not feasible with the volume they receive.

The job application is one of the biggest points of failure in the job search, but it's also one of the biggest opportunities to set yourself apart from other candidates. For many job seekers, this process is one step: fill out and submit the online application. That's why most job applications suck. They do the bare minimum, then blame their résumé for a lack of responses.

What if I told you there's a better way? What if going against the ATS was a choice, and not required? By using the unique application sequence, even if you're filtered out by the ATS for whatever reason (keywords, formatting, etc.), you can bypass it and go straight to a human. The sequence is a multi-stepped approach that will help you strategize how to stand out, how to identify the right person to reach out to, and how to approach them in a way that makes them feel foolish if they don't invite you to an interview.

Step #1: Target One Opportunity

The more narrow your focus, the more effective your efforts will be. The first step is to identify and target *one* company at a time from the list we created earlier. The company may currently be publicly hiring for roles you're interested in, or it may not have current job opportunities open in your role. In either case, you can begin using the unique application sequence. In the latter case, simply focus on the first five steps, using this time to build relationships. This is ideal because once a position is finally available, you'll be in great shape to leverage what you've built.

Step #2: Strategize and Research

Next, strategize your best way to get sponsorship internally by asking yourself: *What is the quickest and most efficient way I can build real trust with this company?*

Being able to establish trust online is a nuanced skill that you can develop with practice, and it's necessary in a world of remote communication. Trust takes time to build but can be lost in a second. Start building it before you submit your application, and continue to cultivate it through the interview phase.

The more research you do, the easier it will be to build trust. Before applying, complete this *Trust Checklist*:

- Follow the company on all social media and start engaging with their content.

- Subscribe to the company communications (newsletters, updates, and so on).

- Set up Google News Alerts and LinkedIn job alerts for the company.

- Identify who you already know in the company or who you know that knows someone in the company.

- Search to see who's active online in the company and posting content, especially on LinkedIn. Follow them and engage with content they post that's relevant to you.

- Browse through the employees at the company and see how you can connect with them on a personal basis (shared interests, clubs, university, etc.).

- Join virtual company events: live streams, user groups, webinars and so on.

- Become a customer of the company when appropriate, even the free version (i.e., buy their product or use their service). Sometimes this may be cost-prohibitive, but especially in software and tech, companies often offer freemium or trial versions of their product.

By doing all of this *before* you apply, you may find an easier route in. You might realize an old colleague you completely forgot about works at the organization. You may discover a recruiter's post about a job you're interested in that encourages applicants to send them a direct message. You may find a webinar being hosted by someone on the team you want to join who you can now meet live during their presentation. The options are endless.

Even by just putting yourself in a position to receive company communication to their customers, you'll have a more well-rounded view of their initiatives and what they want the external world to think about them. Your goal is to implant yourself into their ecosystem to accentuate your understanding of where they're coming from. This becomes powerful because you can speak to specific reference points and use their communications to your advantage. It also helps you confirm whether it's the kind of company you want to work for. This allows you to approach your application with a whole new level of depth that other job seekers won't have.

Step #3: Make a Connection

After developing your strategy and doing research to build trust, it's time to find the easiest and lowest-friction route to make contact within the organization. Before applying, we're aiming to reach out to at least three people. It's tempting to skip this step because it requires more upfront work, but it increases the overall chances of you getting the job. That's the mindset shift: more work upfront to reduce overall work and time in the search overall.

The ideal situation is that you already have an amazing relationship with the hiring manager of your target remote company prior to applying. For most people in most situations, this isn't going to be the case. Therefore, the next rung down is to look for the most relevant employees who have the highest likelihood of responding.

Those at the peer level on the team you want to work on is a good start. Beginning at the equivalent level is usually a lower stakes conversation than starting with a hiring manager, so it can be less pressure. You may also be able to get an introduction to a hiring manager from that person, which carries more weight than reaching out cold. I recommend trying to find someone you currently know who knows somebody at this organization, especially if they are in a relevant role. If you can't get a direct introduction to someone, find a person who's active on LinkedIn (you can view their activity feed) and has some sort of personal relatability to you (similar background, school, interests, etc.). Think again about the lowest barrier of entry with the highest impact. There may not be a *perfect* connection for you based on the criteria I've listed. It's up to you to use your intuition and also reach out to multiple people to increase the chance of response.

If you completed the Trust Checklist, you'll have already identified at least a few. Now is the time to make the connection. Prioritize getting an intro when possible, and when it's not, you can message them about a shared interest, something relatable about your backgrounds, or one of their recent posts. It's even better to warm this up prior to sending a direct message by engaging with their content by liking and leaving thoughtful comments using the 5x5x5 method and perfect comment formula in the networking section of this book. The more personal connection you establish, the better.

The goal is to obtain sponsorship and find someone who will advocate for you internally, pass your résumé forward, get you introduced to someone else, or have some stake in you getting hired. When someone in the organization vouches for you, it creates a level of trust that's unmatched compared to when you apply faceless into the abyss of the internet and ATS.

Step #4: Find the Hiring Manager or a Recruiter

The easiest way to make it through ATS screening is to not deal with it. If you find the hiring manager or a recruiter, you can send your application materials directly to them. You may still be required to submit a standard application, but our goal is to make that part of the process a formality. It's much different when someone is *looking* for your résumé in the system instead of taking the chance they may *find* it in the system. If you were able to make contact with employees at the company in the previous step, try to leverage that relationship to determine who the hiring manager is, and get an intro if possible.

If you don't know who the person hiring for the job is, you can also find an internal recruiter who hires for that team. Either way, some recon might be required on your part. You want to get this information so you can direct your application in an email to someone specific who has power in the decision-making process.

There are tools out there to help you find someone's email address. These tools may change over time, but at the time of writing this, mailscoop.io or hunter.io are my two favorites. Sometimes, though, this information won't be available, or it's difficult to locate, particularly in companies with large structures. That's why it's so important to try to find peer connections first to help you with this.

I recommend taking a guess and asking something along the lines of, "I'm looking to apply to [role title] and I wanted to ensure I gave myself the best chance possible of standing out. I did some research and found a few people I think might be the right contact for me to reach out to. Is [name] the hiring manager/recruiter for the [role title]?" This tends to be more effective than going to them with no information and asking, "Who is the hiring manager/recruiter for [role title]?" In some cases, a peer connection won't share others' contact info but will offer to pass your application on. That can work too—but as much as possible we want to own the relationships with everyone throughout the process, so don't skip out on the research during this step.

Step #5: Build Your Application Package

After you've had at least a conversation or two with people in the company and have identified the hiring manager or a recruiter you can send your materials directly to, you can officially submit your application on the company's website as well (or wherever they're asking applications be submitted). Do your best on the application, and save your answers somewhere on your computer. Every time you fill out an application, keep your answers. It will save you time in the future when you're being asked similar questions, or if there's an issue submitting, you can just paste them in again.

Most people provide only those things a company explicitly asks for: typically a résumé and an online application. To stand out (like Donaldo in the opening story), also include a *cover letter*, a *video application*, and a *value asset*. Let's break down each piece of the application.

Resources:
Application Package Examples and Templates

For résumé, cover letter, video application, and value asset examples and templates, visit www.theremotejobcoach.com/book-resources.

RÉSUMÉ

Résumés are less important than most job seekers think. The majority spend way too much time tweaking and re-tweaking their résumé, placing the bulk of the weight of their job search's success on this one piece of paper, while actively neglecting activities like personal branding or networking.

I get it though. Adjusting your résumé template, fixing up bullet points, or rewording your skills feels tangible and productive. I just want you to understand that it's only one piece of the puzzle. While our goal is to have a fully optimized, functional résumé, we want the résumé to be a mere formality by the time we're using it. During this chapter you'll learn more about that process, but for now, let's go over the core components of what makes a successful résumé.

MAKE THE BEST STUFF EASY TO FIND

Don't make the most relevant and impressive parts of your résumé difficult to find. If your best achievement is hidden at the bottom of the page, or snuck into a random bullet point in your experience section, you're making it too difficult. Give them everything they need to determine your applicability like you're a waiter at a five-star restaurant serving up a silver platter. Put the best stuff above the fold, at the top of the page, front and center.

You only have about five to ten seconds to impress and keep someone reading. The best way I've found to keep recruiters' and hiring managers' attention is to create a *highlights* section. This is a section at the very top of the résumé that summarizes the most pertinent achievements that are relevant to the requirements of the specific job you are applying for. Curate this highlights section by matching keywords and phrases from the job description to exact metrics and experiences in your career. I also recommend a skills section under that where you feature appropriate *remote* tools and skills mentioned in the job listing. If you don't have remote experience, focus on *virtual* work and anything you've done working across time zones, offices, or with people in different locations.

WRITE COMPELLING BULLET POINTS

I see way too many bullet points on résumés simply describing a menial task that someone did. The issue with that? Anyone can *do* a task without doing it well. When you tell me you've done a task like, say, you oversaw a project building a house for orphans and puppies, but don't give me details, I don't know the outcome. You could be either a successful and selfless hero-philanthropist who has a heart of gold, or the overseer of one of the greatest tragedies of this millennium when the house collapsed shortly after being built.

Well-structured bullets will make it easier for the reader to pull out the important information and understand your impact in very few words. A good bullet is simple; it:

- Starts with strong action verbs: Executed, Established, Produced…

- Focuses on impact and benefit for the company, not just tasks

- Showcases key performance indicators like money and time

In addition, it's good to think about the substance of the bullet and what's packaged in each one for maximum effect. Use this formula as your reference point:

(Skills + *Experience* + *Metrics)*

- Skills – Keywords from job listings that match what you're good at

- Experience – Specific experiences that substantiate your skills

- Metrics – Numbers, percentages, and dollars that substantiate success

CUSTOMIZE FOR EVERY JOB

Tailoring your résumé for every job you apply to is mandatory. You'll have a base, boilerplate résumé for each type of role you're interested in. Once you find a job you want to apply to, you can duplicate this base résumé and begin to make adjustments.

The goal is to prove you put in the effort of reading the job description and researching the role and the company. By creating unique highlights and featuring skills that combine specific, key phrases from the job description with your experience and metrics, you can articulate your strengths in context to the job/company.

Look through the job listing and highlight all the keywords. Also consider looking at the company website for any information about their values and mission. Use the exact same words and phrases they use, mixed in with your accomplishments to make it your own. If they say they're looking for a self-starter, don't say you have initiative and drive; say you're a self-starter. Yes, they mean the same thing, but using the exact language shows you did your research, making you come across as well prepared.

As you're doing the work to customize, one thing I've found helpful is to have the job description and résumé on two different documents, side by side. As a client and I take phrases from the listing, we bold or highlight them on both documents so we can see how much we're actually using directly from what the company is giving us. You can even color code it by highlighting it with different colors to signify different types of categories. After fully customizing your résumé, you can run it through a multitude of online résumé tools that scan for matching accuracy.

COVER LETTER

A great cover letter does five things:

- Successfully introduces you to the hiring manager/recruiter

- Makes a strong case for why you'd be a good fit for the job

- Proves your desire and fit to work at their company

- Fills in any missing data that wasn't included on your résumé

- Gives the hiring manager/recruiter a call to action

If you check off those five boxes, your letter can be a compelling, powerful companion to your résumé.

VIDEO APPLICATION

In early 2020, LinkedIn announced they launched video introductions, where hiring managers can request an intro as part of the hiring process and applicants can respond by video. As more and more companies go remote, I predict they'll continue to use video as an initial qualifier and screening mechanism for applicants. Get comfortable doing video applications, because even if it's not required, you can use it to give you a huge edge in the process.

Think of your video application as an extension of your cover letter and résumé. It's a way to give the company a better look at your personality and energy, and even a preview of what it's like to work with you before meeting. By recording a personalized message, you immediately stand out from other candidates in a dynamic way that a résumé or cover letter can't do for you.

A poor video application can harm you as much as a good one can help you, though. Follow these tips to create the best video application:

- **Practice!** Be willing to be shit before you're good. You'll rarely record something you'll want to use the first time. Every client I've ever worked with has gone through at least five to eight practice runs before sending me something they're willing to have me give feedback on. It's part of the process, so be patient with yourself.

- **Look into the camera.** Our goal is to project confidence, energy, and personality. It's easy to look down, look at yourself, look at your script, or gaze off-camera, but those things don't create a connection or allow your character to shine through. Look directly into the camera, and it will feel like you're actually addressing the person on the other end. You can write out key bullets on a sticky note and put it near your webcam for reference, which can help your eyes stay at the same level.

- **Make it look and sound good.** Follow all the tips in chapter 3 about your video and audio setup. Use a quality webcam if you can, a mic, and be thoughtful about the background as well as the lighting behind the camera.

- **Keep it short.** Keep the video under one minute, thirty seconds. I know it can be tough to succinctly describe yourself and why you're a fit for a job in that amount of time, but people have incredibly short attention spans. Brevity is best.

- **Use your cover letter as a guide.** The points you made in your cover letter are the same points you can make in your video application. *Don't* read your cover letter or bulleted notes word for word. Make it as natural sounding as possible and speak from the heart about why the company resonates with you and what value you can bring.

- **Be personal.** Remember, this video is an opportunity to show parts of you that can't be seen on a static résumé. It brings together nonverbal cues in a way that shows what it might be like to communicate with you, and it can be a good indication of cultural fit. Don't be afraid to bring up parts of your personality or background that align to the specific person or company you're sending this to.

There are many free asynchronous video recording tools you can use for your video application. My favorite at the time of this writing is Loom. As a side benefit, companies often use these types of tools to communicate virtually, so you're preparing yourself to be a better remote employee. As an extra bonus: the more you practice recording videos of yourself, especially for hiring managers, the more natural you'll come across in virtual interviews.

VALUE ASSETS

A value asset isn't just a cherry on top of your application sundae; it's a sprinkle of 23-carat edible gold leaf. Also known as a *Value Validation Project* by my friend Austin Belcak (founder of Cultivated Culture) or a *Show Don't Tell* project by my friend Madeline Mann (founder of Self Made Millennial), a value asset is an application supplement that provides proof of your competency to the right person at the right time. It gives a stakeholder at your target company a sneak peek of what it would be like to work with you, and shows you're willing to go above and beyond to stand out.

A value asset has these characteristics:

- A pitch of value that shows you've done research and understand the company

- Proof you have expertise in a particular topic or role

- A preview of what it would be like to work with you

- A document, presentation, or unique asset that wows the person you send it to

- Customized information or ideas that the company can use even if they don't hire you

The exact format of the value asset is less important than the effort. The nice part is you can reuse a value asset as a template for different target companies. You also don't have to create it from scratch. You can repurpose old work or choose a value asset aligned with something you wanted to do anyway. Here are some examples:

- A 30-60-90 proposal, an outline of your plan for your first 30, 60, and 90 days in a role

- Competitive research, gap analysis, or product ideas for a company to expand

- A report on data for new markets, trends, or places where the company can take advantage

- Mistakes on the company website or in external communication, or suggestions for things they could do better

- Sample of work, either from the past or related to a current initiative the company has (you can search for "what does an intern for [XYZ role] do?" and pick a couple of small things)

- Ideas for types of content (or you can even create the content for them)

Depending on the role you're interested in, look at the responsibilities in the job description and consider the person you're sending the asset to. This will determine what form your value asset takes.

If you're a social media marketer and your job requires creating ads for Facebook, take an hour to generate a mock ad. If you're a UX/UI designer, revamp one of their pages and make suggestions about how to make it easier to navigate. If you're in customer support, submit a support ticket, document what can be improved, and create a short video walkthrough. If you're an executive assistant who also manages email campaigns, sign up for the company newsletter and provide direct feedback about the sequences you receive. The options are only limited by your imagination.

Step #6: Reach Out Directly

After submitting your application online, the ideal situation is to send all of these materials directly by email to the hiring manager as well, letting them know you've applied. The brilliance of this step is that 99.9% of other job seekers aren't doing it. They are typically completing the online application and then stopping there. Even if they do contact the hiring manager, they're likely sending a needy, self-serving message. You, on the other hand, are sending the hiring manager a message of value and making their job easier. They are looking for the right candidate, and you're coming to their door knocking with everything they need to just open the door to find you.

By going above and beyond with your unique application, as well as putting effort into building a direct relationship, your application is much less likely to get lost. I've had numerous clients who, after months of not hearing a peep from any applications, heard back almost 100% of the time using this strategy. Think about it. Most human resources professionals and managers are accustomed to receiving the same low effort submissions day after day, job after job. They are just waiting for someone to be creative to catch their attention and show them why they should hire them. Even if you're not the best fit and they reject you, you're much more likely to get a personal response by using this method, rather than getting ghosted or receiving an automated email rejection.

Now, if you haven't been able to determine who the hiring manager is, you can send it to a recruiter. You can also send it to a peer at the company who offers to pass it along, but the idea is to address someone directly in your materials, so having someone else send it for you is a bit impersonal.

Compose a short email and attach your résumé, cover letter, video application, and value asset. Explain concisely your reason for reaching out, the materials included, the job role you're applying for, who you've already spoken with at the company, and your desire to stand out in the process. Be empathetic to the fact that you may be reaching out to them out of the blue. Be understanding that they may be incredibly busy, but at the same time be confident about your value. Mention that if you don't get a response within a week, you'll reach back out, and set up a reminder in your calendar for a week later so you don't forget.

Then, if you haven't already, connect with your company contact on LinkedIn. Use the "Add Note" feature when connecting and let them know you've sent them an email about your application along with a résumé, video, cover letter, and your desire to put a name to the face. By doing this, you've now covered your bases and given yourself the best chance of them seeing the email.

Step #7: Follow Up

You've followed the unique application sequence, it's been a week… and nothing.

Crickets.

It's frustrating. Keep your composure, it's not something to take personally. Even impressive applications can get buried in inboxes and lost in the shuffle, and there are a million reasons why a company may not be getting back to you. Remember, a job search requires selling yourself, and statistics by the National Sales Executive Association estimate that 80% of sales are made on the fifth to twelfth contact.

Having a salesperson's mindset when it comes to following up on your job search can keep you rooted in reality, decrease your discouragement, and provide you with the perseverance necessary to get a response. That's our goal with each application, is to at least get a response, even if you get a rejection. It's much better to get closure and know you *didn't* make it to the interview stage rather than to sit in limbo.

However, most job seekers mess up this part of the process by doing the following:

- They never follow up for one reason or another, which is insanity.

- When they follow up, instead of using it as another opportunity to stand out, they "check in" on their résumé—the same boring, predictable thing everyone else does.

- They put the company on a pedestal and use timid language, downplaying their own value and losing whatever leverage they had.

Hiring managers and recruiters are looking for the cream of the crop to rise. By following up in a distinct way, you remind them of your presence and give them a reason to choose you.

FOLLOW UP REQUIRED FOR SALES

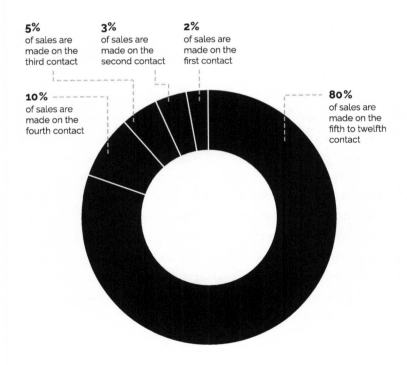

5%
of sales are
made on the
third contact

3%
of sales are
made on the
second contact

2%
of sales are
made on the
first contact

10%
of sales are
made on the
fourth contact

80%
of sales are
made on the
fifth to twelfth
contact

DON'T JUST "CHECK IN"

What most people take for granted in this part of the process is that each micro-interaction matters. Every email, every LinkedIn message, every like or comment, and every small indication of how you act can either be a hindrance or a help in you getting a job. Therefore, with each "check in" on your application, you have a huge opportunity.

The problem is, most job seekers "check in" the same way (that is, if they even follow up at all). Sending the standard "Hi [name], just reaching out to check on my application for XYZ," is passive and timid. It strips you of your leverage and value and implies that you're idly waiting around for a response. This volunteers control of the situation to the person you're sending the message to.

Instead, let's use this opportunity to further demonstrate your value and solidify your competence. Here are some topics you can use during your follow-up to avoid the pitfall of the boring "check in":

- **Send information or ideas highlighting your expertise**—You may have already done a value asset and sent that over to them. You can reference the work you did and add an additional note about your deliverable you can't wait to show them. Really sell why they should have a conversation with you! You can look for interesting industry-specific articles or current events and provide your own commentary on why they might find it interesting. Any way you can highlight your expertise while getting their attention can give you a good opportunity to transition into your application.

- **Personal connection**—Find communities, groups, clubs, universities, and hobbies that you have in common with the hiring manager. Send a note regarding specific information about those communities that they may be able to relate to.

- **Mutual relationship**—Is there someone you know who also knows the hiring manager? You may have already tapped their shoulder to get an intro to this hiring manager, or they may have been the one who told you who the hiring manager was. Ask them a projection question like this, "I submitted my application and sent my materials to [hiring manager] for the [role title]. If you were me, what would you do to get their attention and further myself in the process?" They may offer some interesting solutions you hadn't thought of, or even offer to reach out to the hiring manager for you.

- **Engage with their content**—If the hiring manager for the role is active on LinkedIn, this is a great chance for you to continue to gain familiarity with them. Make sure you're following them and have notifications set up for when they post. Check their activity every few days, and leave thoughtful comments when they post something. Then you can go back to directly messaging them to converse about their post and also bring up your application.

- **Find another medium**—If you've already reached out through email and LinkedIn without response, search the hiring manager's name on Google to find out where else they own social accounts or spend time online. Sometimes people will have a personal website or blog with a contact form, or other social media they're more active on. If you find a place where they're more active, engage there.

You'll notice many of these suggestions are the same networking strategies from *before* the application. Follow-ups are essentially a relationship and trust building activity and require you to continue to show your interest in a unique way, just like you did when you initially applied. Don't let your foot off the gas until you get a response!

Change the Input: Reframe Your Mindset

You're doing a hiring manager a favor.

A lot of people hesitate to reach out to hiring managers because they don't want to be a nuisance. A hiring manager's job is to qualify the best person for the job, so think of it like this: if you're a good fit, and you help the hiring manager hire you, you make their job easier. Therefore, it is your *obligation* to articulate your value, stand out, and give them a reason to hire you and trust you (assuming you can actually do the job). Feel good about that rather than feeling like you're bugging them.

BE A "POLITE PEST"

After applying, put a reminder in your calendar to reach out a week later if you don't get a response by then. Follow up with your other company contacts too, like anyone who gave you an informational interview or peers you're connected with on social media. Try to find backdoors into the company. With each person, space your follow-ups a week apart, and always tell them the next time you're going to be reaching out. If you're a couple of follow-ups deep with a person, add this to your message:

> My intention is to show you I'm persistent and willing to go the extra mile, which is the value I'll also bring to [organization name]. If you're not the right person or you'd like me to stop, please let me know because my intention is not to bother you. Thanks!

If you're bothering them, they'll let you know, and you can stop, but in many instances, you'll find they actually appreciate the perseverance. I know someone who was hired specifically because they kept reaching out and the hiring manager was so tired of it, he figured he might as well give them a chance so they'd stop contacting him. Moral of the story? Show empathy while also going after what you want, the motto of a polite pest.

Step #8: Repeat and Learn As You Go

Repeat this step-by-step process for one to three of your target companies per week. Prioritize quality over quantity. The number you choose depends on how much time and energy you're able to put into creating this caliber of application package. Don't stop networking either. By constantly adding new contacts with your target companies, you can produce opportunities. I've had many clients get jobs *without* applying at all because of their relationships.

Be sure to keep track of everything as you go. Many job seekers who've come to me were applying to hundreds of jobs a month before learning this strategy. They went from that to four to twelve a month, and started getting *more* responses. The benefit for them is that they can actually stay organized now because the sheer volume they were doing before was impossible. By knowing where you stand with each application and company, your job search becomes more digestible and less chaotic. Utilize my Remote Job Search Spreadsheet in the resource library as well as a job searching app to help you track your progress. During the time of writing this, my favorite job search organization tool is called Placement.

Obviously, the ideal situation is that your application and follow-up leads to an interview, but maybe after all your work—building trust, submitting a value-packed application, and following up—the answer you get back is a big, fat no. Yeah, it sucks, but don't take rejection personally. This is true for all things in life.

Stay as detached as possible, and be grateful for *no*s. According to a 2020 LinkedIn survey, 77% of job seekers say they've been ghosted by an employer before. The only thing worse than getting a no is getting no response at all. For every person who takes the time to send you a note explaining you didn't get moved to the next round, be appreciative.

Think of each no as a lesson, a callus that is making you stronger and better, and don't be afraid to solicit feedback. Every no is an opportunity to ask a hiring manager how you can get better and thank them for their time. Use a follow-up like this to gain feedback:

> Hey [hiring manager name], thank you for getting back to me. I wanted to make sure I was able to learn and gain perspective from the experience. How might I become a more desirable candidate for either [XYZ company] or another company in the future? I appreciate all constructive feedback as it's my goal to get better in everything I do. Thank you in advance for your help!

You may not receive a response from this. Again, don't take it personally. Hiring managers often don't have the time or motivation to give feedback. This is one of the best reasons to have a coach who can give you an outside perspective. The *no*s that come with job searches can be discouraging, but keep moving. This is a process. Take what lessons you can, and focus on the next opportunity.

Stand Out and Land the Interview

Remote positions are highly competitive, but by following the unique application sequence, you become different and stand out from the crowd immediately. You'll submit fewer overall applications and have a higher response rate, making you a more effective job seeker. But our work here isn't done yet. Once you get the application sequence to work for you, you'll meet your next exciting hurdle: the interview.

CHAPTER 10

HIT INFO

Preparing for Interviews

VIRGINIA, AN INDONESIAN CITIZEN, WORKED IN THE HOSPITALITY industry in Bali. To some people, living in Bali seems like paradise, but paradise can become a prison if you can't leave. In Virginia's case, she had a dream of traveling the world, but her job required her to be physically present in Bali. She knew a fully remote job was the answer to her conundrum.

At first, she didn't think it was possible for her. Being Indonesian and wanting to work for a US-based tech company, she faced tax and legal hurdles often present for companies that have restrictions in who they can hire. Not to mention, she worried about how her sales skills from the hospitality industry would transfer to tech. She knew she needed some help, and that's when we met.

She went through my course and started implementing the strategies in the networking modules. She was a natural relationship builder. From her experience in sales, she navigated LinkedIn with ease and started targeting employees who worked at fully remote, distributed companies. One of the contacts she got in touch with happened to work for a fully remote tech company that was hiring sales development representatives.

At the time she wasn't even aware they were hiring, but here he was, encouraging her to apply, and offering to get her an interview, all from a cold LinkedIn message.

While she was interviewing, the sales leader she spoke with had concerns about her lack of experience in tech sales. During their time together, she did her best to mitigate his apprehension, but post-interview, she felt a wave of anxiety that it wasn't going to be enough. She came to me and we developed a plan.

After a bit of research, she discovered her interviewer had written a sales book. She ordered it immediately and started reading it. She also completed a quick and affordable online course in tech sales. Then, she created a presentation to address her interviewer's concerns, wrote out a thoughtful plan about how she would gain the necessary experience and knowledge, and outlined the efforts she already committed to since the last time they spoke.

She sent a follow-up email to him requesting to show him this presentation, and mentioned she'd already been reading his book. When her next interview rolled around, she blew him away:

- She made a personal connection with him by sharing notes from what she learned in his book and the course she took.

- She acknowledged his concerns as valid but offered a plan forward while demonstrating she was able to take and use constructive feedback.

- She proved that even though she didn't have all the experience they were looking for, she was willing to learn and put in the work to acquire the skills she needed.

She got the job. Not because of her credentials or experience, but because of how she responded, adapted, and earned trust throughout the interview process. You have a huge opportunity when you interview. It's your chance to hit the info button on the remote and give your interviewer all the information they need to say "Hell yes!" to hiring you, even if you don't have all the checkboxes on paper. The interview also simultaneously gives you the info you need to determine if the job, and more importantly, the company, is a good fit for you too.

Exercises and Resources: Preparing for the Interview

Visit www.theremotejobcoach.com/book-resources for exercises and resources to help you with interviewer and company research, story creation, and interview preparation.

Do Your Research

Your performance in an interview largely depends on what you do *before* the interview. The more prepared you are, the more confident you'll be. Most important of all, when you're confident it's more likely you can show the interviewer the true you, not a nervous, panicked version of yourself.

The purpose of a job interview is to see if there's a *mutual* fit. Oftentimes we think the job provider has all the leverage in these interactions. This isn't the case. You're qualifying them as well. Internalizing this can help shift your sense of the power dynamic and encourage you to do better research, because you're focused on how the company fits what you're looking for. We never want you to make yourself into something you're not just to impress a company. You can mold yourself to fit what they're looking for, but not in a way that's disingenuous to you.

If you've been following my advice so far, you'll already have a good start on your research. If you haven't already completed the Trust Checklist in the "Strategize and Research" section of the previous chapter, do it before heading into your interviews. Sometimes, after completing your research and conducting informational interviews, you may discover the company isn't quite what you were searching for. That's okay! You haven't wasted your time; you've strengthened your criteria and will be better able to identify a remote company and position that checks all the boxes.

Not only is it important to research the company, but the person who will be interviewing you. Companies are made up of humans. The sum of those humans creates the culture of organizations. The person who interviews you is a gatekeeper and a reflection of the type of people that work there. When you can find ways to connect with them on a personal level, they'll be more likely to advocate for you. Check out their LinkedIn and try to find some common ground.

Don't assume you'll remember everything from your research. Take notes, write it down, and even say things aloud. (You can use the Company and Interviewer Research exercises.) Then, before you head into interviews, review all the information you have about the company and role again. It can be easy to think that because you've gone through the exercise of writing things out, you'll remember when it comes time to interview. Review the application you originally sent (including your résumé, cover letter, video application, and any value assets), the job listing and description, any notes from informational interviews, and your research on the interviewer and company.

Tips for Phone and Video Interviews

According to *Psychology Today*, 55% of communication is body language, 38% is the tone of voice, and 7% is actual words spoken. If you're interviewing by phone, you've lost more than half of the communication that takes place in an in-person interview. If you're interviewing by video call, some body language will come across, but not all.

Because of these limitations, strive to give yourself every other advantage possible with these best practices for video and phone interviews:

1. **Smile and breathe deep.** It can feel weird or fake to overly smile, but do it anyway, especially if you're interviewing over the phone. It literally changes how you sound. Smile on video too, but be conscious not to look like a deranged psychopath, which will, understandably, make the interviewer uncomfortable. Find a balance and make it authentic. Let your natural excitement ease into a confident smile while you're talking to them. This will also help your anxiety if you're nervous. Breathing is also nature's remedy of slowing down your nervous system and ridding yourself of tension. Feel yourself take deep, elongated breaths into your nose, through your stomach, up into your chest, and out of your mouth. You don't want it to be overtly loud, but feel yourself fill up with air slowly, as it's easy to clench our muscles and breathe shallowly if we're not aware.

2. **Stand if you can (or sit up straight).** Even if your interviewer can't see your body language, it still impacts how you sound. Standing is a great way to perpetuate confidence and allow your voice to project. When on the phone without video, I highly recommend standing, and when on video, commit to straightening up your posture, or snag a BetterBack, my favorite back support device.

3. **Create a good remote setup.** Follow all the tips from the "Construct the Right Remote Environment" section in chapter 3. Wear headphones or use a mic (or both), and especially

if it's a video interview, hardwire your connection if possible and make sure there's ample light.

4. **Consider what's visible (for video calls).** Remove anything from the background that could be distracting. In the worst-case scenario, an interviewer may form a negative perception based on something they see, subconsciously or otherwise. Avoid controversial or polarizing objects—avoid political signs, drug paraphernalia, or religious symbols. On the flip side, you can also strategically place items in the shot. For example, Jonathan Javier of Wonsulting talked about a story in which he knew his interviewer was a big Star Wars fan. He bought a Yoda AirPods cover and left it visible on his desk. This created a commonality that the interviewer ate up. They spent a substantial amount of time talking about Star Wars, and thus created a deeper personal connection. Subliminal cues like this can work to your advantage if played right.

5. **Find a quiet area.** This cannot be overstated. Find a quiet place in your home, or wherever you're taking the interview. The last thing you want is for the interviewer or yourself to deal with the distraction of noise in the background. Figure out what to do with potential ambulatory distractions, whether kids, dogs, cats, loose guinea pigs, or whatever might interrupt the conversation.

6. **Minimize distractions.** Don't risk the chance of other activities drawing your attention. Keep other devices on airplane mode, and close all tabs on your computer other than your notes or what you need to have in front of you. There's no excuse for not giving your full attention.

7. **Move beforehand.** Five to ten minutes before you jump on the call, do a dance, pushups, jumping jacks, or some kind of movement that will get the blood flowing. Changing your physiology directly influences your emotional state. Nerves and anxiety are akin to excitement; move the energy around and get pumped to nail it.

8. **Keep notes nearby.** One of the big benefits of video or phone interviews is you can have notes without your interviewer realizing it. Have your research and resources in front of you, ready to go. Notes are best in bulleted format so you avoid reading them directly and sound as natural as possible. Use them as reference points, not a gospel.

As with most everything in life, practice is key. Test out these habits while you're on the phone or video chatting with friends and family, and it'll be easier to use these tips with hiring managers and interviewers later.

Change the Input: Reframe Your Mindset

Don't memorize questions. Master your stories.

People often approach a job interview like a test in school. They think if they can get a copy of the test, they can memorize all the questions and answers and get an A. It doesn't work that way in an interview. First, it's impossible to memorize all the potential questions you'll be asked. Yes, some interview questions come up regularly, but you can never know for certain what will happen. You want to be able to react and adapt when an interviewer throws a curveball you didn't expect. Second, memorized answers can come across stiff and leave little room for you to connect with the interviewer.

When you master and internalize your stories, you can acclimatize them for any number of questions and become flexible enough to handle whatever comes your way. It's also less work for you overall. Instead of memorizing dozens of questions, you can focus on a handful of impactful stories, adjusting them to meet the needs of each question.

Become a Storyteller: The STAR Method of Answering

Now it's time to get into the meat of the interview: question and answer—or, more accurately, story time. Humans love stories. It's how we understand things. Even beyond interviews, everything comes back to story—it's how you gain influence, connect with others, and have better relationships, professionally and personally. In an interview, you will make your case for why you should be hired with stories about your past experience or what you'd do in a hypothetical situation.

Prep stories for your interview ahead of time. Use the Skills Reflection exercise mentioned in chapter 4 (and available in the resource library) for ideas about what could be specifically used for the role you're interviewing for. Take keywords and phrases in the responsibilities and requirements sections of the original job listing, and map these to relevant achievements or accomplishments you listed in your Skills Reflection. By combining their exact words and your unique metrics and experiences, you'll be able to create relevant and powerful stories. You can make a list of these stories in your Remote Job Search Spreadsheet (also available in the resource library).

Make these stories multifunctional and applicable to a multitude of behavioral or situational questions. For instance, maybe you have a story about a time a client was upset but you worked across departments to fix their problem. That story could be used to demonstrate problem-solving ability, innovation, teamwork and collaboration, customer service skills, or a number of other skills and traits your interviewer is looking for.

Think of all the possible applications when creating a story and tease out different versions based on those angles.

If you're struggling to brainstorm story ideas, it can help to look up common interview questions and think of stories you could use as answers. I've included some in the resource library, and you can also check out websites like Glassdoor to find information from other job candidates about the questions asked in interviews. However, the goal isn't to be tied to these questions, only to use them as a resource to create highly functional stories.

How you tell your stories is as important as the stories themselves. Telling stories in a way that's not only concise but also impactful can be difficult. The STAR method by DDI can help. The simple components are as follows:

- **Situation/Task**: Share the context of the situation and overview of the task. This lead-in functions as a broad, high-level answer and helps frame what to listen for in the story.

- **Action**: Give specific details about what you and anyone else involved did in the moment to handle the situation.

- **Result**: Talk about the impact and quantify with metrics and key performance indicators whenever possible, focusing on the value for the company.

After writing these out, *practice*! When you recite a story as an answer during an interview, you don't want it to be your first time saying it aloud. Remember: The idea is NOT to memorize answers to questions, but to get comfortable reciting your stories with a natural flow. As you practice, remove your notes and only use bullet points with one or two words as your reminder. Eventually, your stories will lock into your subconscious. You want to be able to visualize the moments of each story happening sequentially in your brain like they were word pictures. Once you master the structure, it will start to get easier and easier. (Check out the resource library for examples of good and bad answers as well as templates for responding to questions.)

With preparation and practice, you'll have great stories ready to go and a natural, smooth rhythm to your answers during the job interview.

Pro Tip: Record Your Practice for Feedback

Practicing your stories before your interview goes a long way. Take things to the next level by recording yourself. This way you can watch yourself back and analyze not just the story, but your body language and tone (which, remember, make up the majority of communication). You can also send the recording to someone you trust for feedback, like a coach! This kind of feedback is something I do for my clients that provides massive insights. Don't underestimate the power of an outside perspective.

Advanced Interview Tips

Using stories and the STAR method will give you a solid foundation for your interview, but we're not striving for good; we're striving for *great*. Go above and beyond with these advanced interview tips:

1. **Use their keywords and phrases.** I've mentioned it before and I'm mentioning it again so you understand the importance of this point. You might not know the exact questions your interviewer will ask, but you *do* know what the company is looking for. It's right there in the language they use. Search the job description and company website for keywords and phrases that you can sprinkle throughout your stories. You can use these keywords as anchors for your responses. Attach a

story to each keyword or phrase that resonates with you. Then when you use a certain keyword, it will be a cue or trigger to also bring up a particular story.

2. **Add your interviewer's experience into your answers.** Bring the interviewer into your answers when possible. For example, maybe you're switching industries, and you know from your research that your interviewer also switched industries to join the team. If your interviewer asks how you think you'll be able to transfer your skills, you can explain how you think it will work for you, then say something like, "[name of interviewer], I noticed you also switched industries to land where you did with [company name]. What do you think are the reasons you've been so successful?" Once they've given you their answer, you now have additional ammunition to add to your own response because the reasons they were successful might apply to you too.

3. **Don't overemphasize your desire to be remote.** I brought this up as a common application mistake, and it's a mistake in interviews too. Remote work might be a topic of discussion during the interview and it's certainly fine to highlight your remote skills, any experience working remotely that you have, and tools you've used for remote collaboration. My recommendation, however, is to focus more on why you're competent for the role itself without putting the idea of being remote on a pedestal. If they can sense that you're desperate about being remote as opposed to sensing your compatibility with the job, that could be an issue. Remember, especially for remote-first companies, remote work is just *work*. Because it's the default, it's almost assumed that working remotely isn't this huge deal, it's just part of the gig.

4. **Ask great questions.** A true test of a job interview is the
    questions *you* ask. Job interviewers are judging you based on
    these questions because it indicates how much research you've
    done, how creative you are, and what's important to you. Ask
    thought-provoking questions that display your knowledge of
    the company and the role and actually get you the answers you
    need to know if it's a good fit. (Go to the resource library for
    examples.) Don't ask yes or no questions, or anything you can
    easily find the answer to online. Focus on unique, open-ended
    inquiries that serve to gain the opinion of the interviewer.

5. **When presented with an objection, reframe it as an oppor-
    tunity.** If a company or hiring manager indicates a concern
    about your experience or skills, the interview is the perfect place
    for you to address it. Be proactive and show them how you've
    already begun taking steps to address their concern, and how
    this issue is actually an opportunity. Refer back to Virginia at
    the beginning of the chapter as an example.

6. **Get contact information and clarify next steps.** The key to
    the end of the interview is to get the next steps and the contact
    information you'll need to follow up. Not having contact info of
    an interviewer, especially during a panel where multiple people
    are present, will make follow-up less personal. You want to be
    able to individually send out thank you notes afterwards. Get
    clarity on the next steps of the process, when you can expect
    to hear something, and any other info that will assist you in
    creating valuable touch points in between. Once you've got this
    intel, you can add a note in your calendar as a follow-up date
    in case you don't hear back.

The Post-Interview Trick to Success

You've made it through the interview in one piece. Maybe you're thrilled with how it went. Maybe you're kicking yourself for fumbling your answers like Kevin from *The Office* dropping his pot of famous chili. Either way, following up is your mandatory duty to advance the process forward and give yourself the best chance of moving to the next round.

As I mentioned in the application section, so many people complete an application and don't follow up. Somehow I see the same trend with interviews. Job seekers will go through the process of interviewing or screening with an interviewer and will just sit back and wait for an answer. Don't be that person.

The company has invested the time and resources to interview you. They were interested enough to do that. That's an investment neither of you can get back, and you owe it to yourself to get an answer—whether it be a yes or no, just like the application process.

THE FIRST FOLLOW-UP

Immediately after an interview, send a follow-up email to all those who interviewed you. The ideal situation is to send individualized messages if there were multiple people. If for some reason you didn't confirm each specific contact, you can send one email to the person who contacted you about the interview, and ask them to forward it to the relevant individual(s).

Use this email to accomplish a few important things:

- Thank them for their time.

- Show your proactivity and that you want the position.

- Recap valuable parts of the interview.

- Reinforce why you're a great candidate for the role.

- Address any concerns in the interview or clarifications you want to make.

Once you send this email out, add your interviewers on LinkedIn if you haven't yet. Always choose to "Add Note," sending a quick thanks for their time, and referencing that you just sent over an email.

Reinforcing your proactivity immediately after an interview will create a massively good impression with the company. And time matters. If you and another candidate are equal in many ways, they might judge based on who had the best and most effective follow-up, because it provides them with a tangible action you took to show them you want it more.

THE SECOND FOLLOW-UP

You can't expect to be someone else's priority. Hiring managers and interviewers have a lot going on. Sometimes things fall through the cracks, and other times filling your job role may be pushed to the back burner as people take care of the necessities of everyday business. Don't take this personally! If you don't hear back, give them the benefit of the doubt, and send your second follow-up.

You asked for the next steps during the interview process. Now it's time to hold them accountable to their word. By following up and reaching out, you're helping them stay on top of their tasks. They will appreciate that!

Let's say the hiring manager said they would get back to you by Monday the 14th. If you haven't heard anything by the 15th, shoot over an email. Reuse the strategies from the previous chapter (in "Step #7: Follow Up") to follow up in a unique way. Do something to stay top of mind, like including an experience you didn't bring up in the interview that relates to the role, or emailing them a valuable piece of content relevant to your conversation. Remember, the less you're just checking in and the more you're proving you're ready to take on the world, the better. Give them an abundance of reasons to choose you, and continue this process until you hear back.

WHAT IF YOU GET REJECTED?

Getting rejected hurts, especially at this stage. If you made it to an interview, you were likely excited at the chance to get an offer, and it's easy to become attached to the idea of working for a certain company. Once rejection hits, you might be plagued by limiting beliefs, thoughts that you're not good enough, or other dramatic stories our minds love to hyperfocus on. Avoid being dragged down in negativity. Getting a job is a lot like dating. Sometimes the fit isn't right, and that doesn't mean there's something horribly wrong with you and you'll never find your match. Keep working on yourself and you'll attract the right opportunity.

We often sensationalize the job search process and underestimate how much work, effort, and time certain results take to achieve. Getting a remote job is a process, not an overnight attainment. Practice patience and practicality. Push through difficult times because it's the people who commit to finding a job through the struggle that actually get what they want.

If you're rejected, receive it gracefully and learn from it. Just by making it through interviews, you've already gained valuable practice and lessons. Send an email to get additional feedback. (You can use the same script from the last chapter about getting feedback after a rejected application.)

Yes, getting rejected sucks. But the sooner you pick yourself back up and move forward, the sooner the universe will reward you for getting back in the game.

Crush Your Interview

Landing an interview with a remote company is a monumental achievement for many job seekers I work with. Especially for those who are conditioned to receive silence or apply to hundreds of positions without success, this is something to celebrate. But you're not out of the woods yet. The work is just beginning. It's crucial you're highly prepared to put yourself in the best position to succeed, because failing to prepare is preparing to fail. You've made it this far in the book, so I know you're committed to being in the top 1% of job seekers who put in the work.

If interviews fill you with anxiety, don't trip. With some education and practice, you can feel more confident and crush your interview.

CHAPTER 11

SEARCH AND SELECT

Living and Working Abroad

ON MARCH 3, 2018, I LEFT THE UNITED STATES FOR MY FIRST EXTENDED period of *digital nomadism*. I'd been remote in the United States since 2013, and I'd traveled to Thailand and Mexico for vacation, but I'd never lived and worked abroad like this. I was on a trip with a Remote Year program—visiting four different countries in four months with fifty strangers. Everything was going to be new: the cultures, people, food, and ways of living.

I'd recently departed a long-term relationship, quit my job at a small public relations firm, and decided to leave Portland, Oregon, where I'd been living for a number of years. Along with the savings I'd built up, I was supporting myself with some freelance work, the inception of my first coaching programs, and also knew I eventually wanted to work at Remote Year. It was a beautiful disaster, and I was fully embracing the uncertainty ahead of me.

The first stop was Lisbon, Portugal, and to double down on re-modeling my life, I'd taken on the challenge of running my first half marathon in Lisbon in March, followed by my first full marathon in the Czech Republic, two months later. This is coming from a guy who hated running most of his life, so I was well outside of my comfort zone. A few years earlier I couldn't even run one mile at a time, so Lisbon was a hell of a place to start. With rolling hills, slick limestone sidewalks, and tight streets, my five- to ten-mile trots mostly consisted of me dodging little European cars I'd never seen before and trying not to eat shit in front of a cute Portuguese girl who might've glanced my way.

Nonetheless, I had to train for the upcoming races. It was the day after I'd arrived, and I went out for my first run. I found a pedestrian path along the Tagus River and followed it toward a monument that looked familiar: the Ponte 25 de Abril Bridge. If you've ever seen the bridge, you might notice something interesting. It looks exactly like the Golden Gate Bridge in San Francisco, just across the bay, about forty minutes from where I was born and raised. In fact, Lisbon and San Francisco are considered sister cities because of the similarities in their hills, cable cars, and bridges.

As I ran up to the bridge, I admired my surroundings. Besides a few people in restaurants about a half-mile away, I was alone, and the murmurs of conversations and the music from the eateries faded away in the background. The sun was slightly peeking out over scattered clouds, providing an iridescent glow off the water as it gently splashed upon the bank. I was now directly under the bridge, staring at this massive, orange structure, wondering how the hell architecture of this magnitude was built in the sixties. I felt totally lost in the world, in a different country, surrounded by a different culture and people speaking a different language, yet here I was, underneath this bridge that felt so familiar. I was struck with this sense of *home,* across an ocean, away in a foreign country. How could I be so *lost*, yet feel so *found*?

I realized that the sense of home I found in that moment was internal, and I was overcome with a feeling of liberation. I didn't realize how disconnected I'd been feeling in my life previously. Disconnected from my purpose, disconnected from my romantic relationships, my friends, my family, my job, everything. But something clicked. All I'd done up until that moment, the obstacles I'd overcome—subleasing my apartment, getting through my breakup, leaving my job and the US, finding freelance work, starting a coaching business, and a thousand other details to get to this point—led to me here, now, standing under this bridge. I was exactly who I wanted to be, where I wanted to be, doing what I wanted to do, and no external force could persuade me otherwise. *I fucking did it*, I thought.

The distinct and ethereal chord that struck my soul that day was transcendent. It propels me to this day to do what I do in helping others find remote work. I don't care what other people want to do with their lives, whether they work from home, travel the world, or just spend more time with their family. What I care about is helping them find that lightning rod moment of clarity and liberation for themselves. To feel the freedom and sovereignty that forever changed me and what I believed was possible.

For me, this was only the beginning. By the end of the year, I had lived for at least a month or more in Split, Croatia; Prague, Czech Republic; Cape Town, South Africa; and Mexico City, Mexico. Each place brought its own lessons and became part of my identity. I've continued to travel the world and work abroad since 2018, and obtained residency in Mexico. Working abroad was my way of "searching and selecting" the right place for my ideal lifestyle. By having the ability to be intentional in choosing where I wanted to live abroad, I gained new perspectives and ways of thinking about myself and the world.

The Allure of Working Abroad

Traveling and working abroad isn't for everyone, but it's one of the most common reasons people want to work remotely. I understand why. I lived in over fifteen countries on five continents from 2018 to 2022, and nothing has had a greater impact on my life.

When I first started traveling, I thought the main point of my journey would be to learn about all these different countries and people—which I certainly did. Over time, I realized it was actually about me learning about myself. Gaining insight into other cultures and people is powerful and rewarding in its own right, but these insights then serve as reference points for your own self-perception and self-awareness. You grow and stretch, no longer confined to the box of your own upbringing and culture.

Traveling can help you figure out what's important because it's constantly exposing you to cultural practices and belief systems different from yours. Some might resonate, some might not, but perhaps you'll end up incorporating new customs, perspectives, routines, or rituals into your life as a result. I had a rude awakening when I first started living in Mexico, and I realized that for as much as I thought I was a pretty chill and easygoing person, I've been conditioned not to be. My expectation for service providers is to have things done fast. My expectation for meeting people is that they're on time. My expectation for waitstaff is that they are overattentive.

I realized how much the United States values and promotes hustle culture and *doing* rather than just *being*. But then I land in Mexico and everyone's just, well, *chill*. They live much slower. They have more patience. They value family and relationships over work. It immediately challenged my core beliefs and identity because I was forced to adjust my worldview of what was important. Experiencing this contrast made me a better person. While I still respect the grind and appreciate timeliness, my expectations, demeanor, and outlook have changed. I now prioritize rest, relaxation, and slower living because it nourishes me.

Other cultural differences may reinforce or solidify your opinions. In many countries in Europe, for instance, they eat dinner late—like sitting down and stuffing themselves with bread and wine at eleven o'clock at night, late. It literally blows my mind. I'm already in bed an hour before dinner even starts having nightmares about their digestive systems. When I was in Lisbon for that first month of international travel, I had Uber Eats on speed dial because I was tired of the scrutiny and side-eyes from waitresses when I would go to a restaurant before 8:00 p.m. and ask them for a menu. Not every cultural norm is meant for you to adopt.

In the simplest terms, when you travel and work abroad, you get connected to the world, and you get connected to yourself.

Like remote work itself, though, working abroad isn't a be-all and end-all solution. You're not automatically going to feel fulfilled because you're working from the white-sanded beaches of the Caribbean instead of your home country. The heat can be miserable (today I sweat through three shirts), the maintenance guys are usually a day or two late, and if you have a weak stomach, you'll be in for some nights hugging the porcelain throne. Remember, location independence does not equal location ambiguity. The goal is to make an intentional choice about where to live once you attain the independence to do so. Whether working abroad is right for you—and *how* you work abroad—will depend on your vision for your life.

Different Ways to Work Remote while Abroad

Working remotely while abroad can mean a lot of different things. There's no standardization around terms for different types of digital nomads, but the closest I found was a tweet by Andreas Klinger, former head of remote at Angel.co, CTO at On Deck, and founder of Remote First Capital, who breaks it down like this:

- **Digital tourists (what Klinger calls "workstation tourists")**—These individuals want to travel but can't take time off of work to do so, like a CEO who can't step away from the business or someone who has already used up all their vacation time. So they combine vacation and work. They travel to another country for a week or two and work remotely, and then in their off-work hours, they get to be a tourist.

- **Digital backpackers**—These people want to see the world on a bigger scale than workstation tourists. They move location frequently, usually every one to three weeks, and they often travel on a budget. Because they move around a lot, they require great flexibility in their work schedule. They often own their own business or work as freelancers or influencers.

- **Digital slowmads**—Beyond *seeing* the world, these individuals want to *experience* it. They stay in a single location for a longer period of time, typically one to six months. They try to get a bit more involved in the local community. Because they're in the same place for a while, a greater variety of remote positions can lend themselves to this style of working abroad.

- **Digital expats (what Klinger calls "remote workers")**—These people live long-term in another country, becoming fully immersed in the local culture and community. They stay in a single place for longer than six months. They can create and optimize their daily routine for their own needs, so they can do almost any kind of remote work, as long as it doesn't have geo-restrictions.

Resource: Digital Nomad Visas

More and more countries are offering *digital nomad visas* to attract remote workers. It's a fascinating and important development in the legalization of remote work, but unpacking these visas extends beyond the scope of this book. If you're interested in digital nomad visas—what they are, what countries offer them, and how to get one—visit www.theremotejobcoach.com/book-resources for more information as these are constantly updating.

As far as visas and legalities, these terms are not official designations, they're just a way to categorize different lifestyles that people choose. The style that works best for you will vary depending on your circumstances and priorities, and you may find you transition from one style to another. I started off traveling with Remote Year one month in a country at a time (what could be considered a digital slowmad) and then transitioned to living for years in Mexico with my residency (could be considered digital expat).

In general I prefer to have a more established routine that helps me focus on work, so I've realized that multiple months in a country is typically my minimum. At the time of writing this I've been planning my year in quarters. This means a few months at a time in my favorite places, a few months with my family, and a few months exploring new destinations. There are no rules to this and it will likely continue to change for me with time, and of course, when I meet my future wife, who's probably reading this. Whatever style you opt for, be prepared for what I think is the biggest challenge of working abroad: integrating work and life.

Remote Travel Organizations and Communities

Leveraging communities designed to help remote workers and nomads can fast-track your success working abroad. As mentioned previously in the book, I first started my journey overseas with a company called Remote Year. They curate trips of varying lengths to bring together groups of people who already work remotely, while taking care of the logistical hassle of getting set up in a new city (coworking, apartment, transit to and from the airport, etc.). You also end up with a built-in network of remote workers and travelers, which has provided me with some of my closest friends.

In addition to organizations that take care of logistics for you, there are also many that focus on a virtual support system, often facilitating meetups and conferences throughout the year. I've been part of Nomad Cruise/NomadBase, Nomad List, and the Dynamite Circle, which have all greatly impacted my life. This only scratches the surface of the types of supportive communities that are out there for you to choose from, and as digital nomadism continues to boom, we'll only see more and more pop up.

The Integration of Work and Life

At the start of working abroad, there's often a honeymoon phase, where work goes by the wayside. At least, that was the case for me. When traveling with Remote Year, one of my greatest challenges was being effective and performing at the top level for myself and my business. There were so many new places to see and exciting things to do. I was so distracted and all over the place, it was like I was hunting lizards with sticks. I felt a false sense of urgency—FOMO (fear of missing out), where I thought I had to go everywhere and do everything *immediately*.

If you fall into the FOMO trap and spend all your time playing instead of working, your job performance will suffer. That's a major issue, because it could cause you to lose your job. No job equals no working abroad, and then you *will* start missing out.

On the other side of the spectrum, I had periods where I buried myself in my work, out of a sense of insecurity: *This could end at any moment if I don't work hard enough.* I worked so much I wasn't enjoying the travel or exploring the incredible places around me. Other people even noticed and made comments about how I was always working. That's an easy way to burn out, and what's the point of working abroad if you don't take advantage of being abroad?

Working abroad requires integration, incorporating both work and life into one. Integration is about embracing JOMO—the *joy* of missing out. When you understand what's non-negotiable to you and what's leaking your energy, you can prioritize with intention. You don't mind missing out on everything else because it's missing out that allows you to do and experience what matters most.

What integration looks like for you will constantly change as you learn more about yourself and discover new things you want and things you could do better. To maintain integration, I recommend engaging in daily, weekly, monthly, and yearly reflection.

Change the Input: Reframe Your Mindset

Working Abroad ≠ Vacation

Getting away from the grind for a week or two creates the perfect storm of justification for alcoholic binges, sugar rushes, skipped gym days, and the induction of laziness in epic proportions. That's fine, because vacations end. Eventually after a few hangover days and archiving thousands of missed emails, you get back in the saddle of normality.

What happens, though, when you're traveling to an exotic location that other people only dream of vacationing to, and you expect yourself to work? What if every time you step outside of your apartment, the lure of Michelin star restaurants, flaming cocktails, or hidden waterfalls are beckoning, but you've got client meetings all day?

Working abroad long-term requires a different mindset, which means overcoming years of FOMO conditioning and all the excuses that have been programmed into your brain to tell you, "We're in a different country. You have to try this food! You have to drink this drink! You have to see this sight!" Our goal is to create a sustainable *lifestyle*, not a vacation. If you treat working abroad like a vacation, you'll be building your remote lifestyle on a foundation of sand.

From Hard Work Comes Great Rewards

Working remotely while traveling abroad can be one of the most rewarding, enriching experiences of your life. But enjoying those benefits requires being effective in your job, because it's simultaneously the thing that enables you to take advantage of the opportunity. So focus on integration and be willing to put in the hard work for the lifestyle you want.

Resource: Habits of Highly Effective Nomads

Working as a digital nomad comes with unique challenges. Based on interviews with hundreds of these nomads from around the world and my own experiences, I've identified some common habits among highly effective nomads. Visit www.theremotejobcoach.com/book-resources for a breakdown of these habits and tips to sustain a more successful and fruitful nomadic life.

CHAPTER 12

SKIP FORWARD TO YOUR FUTURE

Get Help and Go Faster

WE'VE COVERED A LOT IN THIS BOOK! IF YOU'RE FEELING OVERWHELMED, I get it. Since you've already heard plenty from me, here's advice from some of my clients, who have been where you are right now—excited about working remotely but perhaps feeling a bit overwhelmed—and pushed through it to build the life they wanted:

- **Virginia:** "If you're at a point where clearly what you're doing hasn't worked, you need to realize that if you keep doing the same thing, it's never going to change."

- **Lexi:** "I look back a year ago, and I was miserable in my nine-to-five office job, and taking that one step [of investing in myself and my remote job search] really, really changed my life."

- **Mariel:** "You have to want it so bad within yourself, so bad that it hurts you. Job searching can be daunting. It's changed so much in the past decade. It's so much more than just applying for a job."

- **Joe:** "It's all about investing in yourself, working with someone who you can trust that has shown success with others."

Finding remote work can be a lengthy and challenging process, but it's worth it. Fortunately, there are ways you can hit the skip button to jump ahead, so you can be more effective in your job search and achieve your vision faster.

Change the Input: Reframe Your Mindset

Assumptions become self-fulfilling prophecies.

When we assume causation, we create blockages. Let me explain. If you've failed before in a remote job search, or have certain assumptions about remote companies, your abilities, or why people haven't responded to you in the past, that belief will obstruct new, contradicting information. By not considering new data that would force you to refute your convictions, you'll stay stuck in the same cycle of results, and ultimately, you manifest the exact negative outcome you assumed would happen.

Any number of assumptions could be holding you back, but the assumption of failure is the most deadly. This is where having an outside perspective is valuable. If you've been conditioned to expect failure, you may be too close to even realize how that mindset is dominating your perception of reality. You don't have to be alone in this job search. You don't have to start from scratch and recreate the wheel. You can learn from and lean on others to help you get through this to your goal.

You Are Your Greatest Investment

If you take away only one thing from this book, let it be this: *invest in yourself*—in your career, your skills, and your well-being. It's the wisest investment you can make.

Before you tell me you don't have the resources or time to invest in yourself, let me point out that you're already investing in something. You are spending your time, your energy, and your money on *something*, but is that something improving your life?

Look at your calendar and what you actually do during the day. If you had to, could you account for every minute, or even hour, truthfully? How much time do you spend playing on your phone or deciding what to watch on Netflix? How much of your time is spent bettering your career? Learning new skills so you can get the remote job you want? Improving your health? Nurturing your relationships? Whatever your time breakdown is, are you happy with it?

How about your energy? How much energy do you expend on moving closer to your dreams, and how much do you devote to a job you hate? And your money? Obviously we all have financial necessities in life—rent, groceries, bills. But when it comes to your disposable income, how much do you spend on furthering your goals, and how much do you spend chasing fleeting bursts of dopamine?

All the tips and strategies I've shared in this book *work*. But it's a requirement to put in the time and energy to make it happen. I promise, I don't say this with a condescending tone. I only say it because I run across a plethora of job seekers who lie to themselves about how much they're working toward their dreams. I'm not here to baby them, or you, for that matter. Either you're investing in yourself and getting better, or you're not. I'm putting on my televangelist hat for a moment, because this is a come-to-Jesus moment. If you want to spend hours every day scrolling social media, watching TV, and playing video games, that's fine. But don't complain about how you can't find a remote job if that's the case.

Dive Deep with Courses, Content, and Coaching

Throughout this book, I've done my best to equip you with all the tools and strategies you need to land a remote job. The reality is, there's only so much a book can do, and even if you're armed with knowledge, the job search process can be overwhelming. *You don't need to do it alone.* There's a wealth of resources out there, and a number of ways you can invest in yourself, including helpful content, courses, and coaches that can help you reach your goals.

At a minimum, exhaust the digital resources and exercises I've provided throughout the book. They can help you translate the concepts and strategies into action. Look into courses and coaching, as well. At the time of writing this, I offer both, and if my book resonated with you, then so will these paths. Who knows what the future will bring, though? I likely won't coach people on how to find remote jobs forever. I have other visions and dreams I'm working toward myself, like becoming a film director, university professor, real estate mogul, and father, among other things. There are an abundance of qualified and experienced coaches out there, so if I'm not offering coaching options by the time you've picked up this book, don't let that be an excuse for not getting help.

I walk the walk regarding my recommendation to invest in oneself. Whenever I need to upgrade my skills, I hire experts to help me. It's like surrounding myself with an all-star team in all aspects of my life, and each one shares some of the load we're carrying up the mountain together. I've hired business coaches, basketball trainers, ukulele instructors, tantra masters, and even publishing experts to help me write this book you're reading now (thanks, Scribe Media). My investments in others to help me get to where I want to go personally and professionally have easily surpassed $50,000 in the past year and will likely continue to grow as I continue to level up. I'm not saying you need to do that. I just want you to get a real indication of how much I believe in asking for and receiving help.

There are a lot of benefits to working with an expert:

- **Organization and accountability**—They can help you create your plan and stick to it. When you have only yourself to hold you accountable, it's easy to come up with excuses and put off doing the work necessary to accomplish your vision. Hiring a coach or enrolling in a course will help keep you on schedule.

- **Networking**—You know how critical relationship building is to getting a remote job. One of the biggest benefits of having a coach is gaining access to their network. With several of my clients, like Kelly (from chapter 7), I had someone in my network who worked at the company they were interested in and was able to set up an introduction.

- **Confidence**—When you recruit an expert for your job search, your confidence shifts. When I hired my marketing coach, I felt the shift immediately. I went from uncertainty and doubt to *knowing* I could do it, because I now had an expert on my side.

- **Collaborative brainstorming**—It is so easy to get in your head when searching for a job. You start to question your decisions and run into walls where you have no idea what to do next. Having an expert to bounce ideas off of and brainstorm is invaluable.

Finding the right person to work with can be a challenge, though. Choose carefully to get the most out of your investment:

- **Go niche—find someone who's done what you want to do.** If you have a specific goal, it makes sense to get a specialized expert. When I wanted to learn how to use my task management software and then my course platform (two separate pieces of tech), I found two different coaches that specialized in each one to help me.

- **Ask your network.** When I'm looking for an expert, I start with my network, so I can solicit a trusted recommendation first. If I can't find a suggestion from someone I know personally, I'll ask in online communities related to the niche I'm interested in.

- **Look for people producing valuable content.** This is how I found my marketing coach, Colin. I wanted to learn more about video creation, and when I searched YouTube about a marketing concept I wanted to learn more about, his video popped up near the top. I figured if he was showing up that high in the algorithm he was doing something right. The quality of the video was astounding. I liked his vibe, found his content helpful, and watched a bunch of his testimonials. It was an easy decision.

- **Get someone who believes in what they're doing.** A coach who doesn't have a coach or a course instructor who doesn't take courses is like a personal trainer who doesn't work out or a dietitian who only eats McDonalds. If they believe in what they're doing, it will be easy to tell how they incorporate it in their own life as well.

If you care about your career, if you care about your life, if you care about developing yourself, investing in content, courses, and coaching is just the obvious choice to me. Limit the excuses and put your time, energy, and money into what truly matters.

Find Your People—Remote Communities

Remote communities are another great resource. In chapter 7, we already discussed how you can use communities to build relationships and get closer to your target personas. Not only are communities a way to broaden and deepen your network, but they can help you stay motivated and inspired during the job search. You can share in the celebration of your and others' successes, commiserate over shared challenges, and learn new techniques and strategies for your search.

Finding the right communities is a lot like finding the right expert. Be targeted. If you can find communities specific to your industry, your role, or whatever you're interested in (e.g., working remote), they will probably be more helpful to you than general groups. Asking your network for suggestions can lead you to great groups, as can searching for where valuable content is being posted.

Resist the urge to join all the communities you find. If you spread your attention too thin, it will be too difficult to extract value and contribute at the level you want to. Instead, only join the few you see as the most helpful or best fit for you.

Resource: Find Remote Jobs for You

Visit www.theremotejobcoach.com/book-resources for the Find Remote Jobs for You resource (also referenced in chapter 6), which has a section with several dozen remote job communities, including industry-specific options.

Commit to Your Job Search, Your Vision, and Yourself

Information is one thing; action is another. If information alone hasn't motivated you to take action in your remote job search, it helps to surround yourself with experts and a community. In addition to all the knowledge and expertise you can gain from coaching and communities, making this investment in yourself is a clear act of commitment.

Opportunities that were previously dormant suddenly open up to you. Your eyes can finally witness all the abundance surrounding you because you're willing to finally see it. It's time to commit—to your job search, your vision, and yourself.

CONCLUSION

I WAS IN TULUM FOR THE SELINA MEXICO NOMADS ROAD TRIP IN 2019. Twelve of us won a competition for an all-inclusive trip to seven different Selina hostels across Mexico. It was a dreamlike situation.

Their Tulum location was new at the time, right on the water, and was closed to the public. We checked into our untouched rooms, put our stuff down, and on cue, it started pouring rain. Like fat, heavy drops. The ones that feel like tiny paintballs. I sat down at the desk in my room and opened my computer. I figured I'd get some work done with the ambience of the precipitation pelting the window above me.

As I was sifting through emails, I began to feel an uncompromising urge to get up. I couldn't focus, and the screen no longer appeared inviting. I wanted to go for a run. Over a year earlier, when I started running marathons, I promised myself that if I ever felt the intuitive calling to run, I wouldn't ask myself any questions or overthink it. I'd simply lace up my Nikes, pop on some headphones, and just do it. But this time was different. Where my instincts were directing me, there was no need for shoes or music.

I popped on my bathing suit and took a few steps out of my room to peer down the stretch of white sand. It looked like it went on forever. I carried only my room key in a velcro pocket and walked out to the beach, barefooted as a yard dog. Water was falling in sheets. Within a few steps it looked like I had fallen into a pool, but in the Tulum heat, every drizzle was refreshing. With sideways rain smacking my back, I embarked down the shoreline with a light jog.

Throughout my life, I've been conditioned to avoid rain as much as possible. Whether it was hearing people complain about getting soaked, my parents' insistence on me wearing a jacket to stay dry, or offhand comments about bringing an umbrella, I'd internalized that it was best to stay dry when it rained. But here I was, traversing the coastline of a Mexican paradise during the preliminary stages of a hurricane, grinning wide-eyed as a toddler after tasting their favorite candy. My feet splashed in the shallowest part of the ocean where the tide meets the sand, and as I looked around, there wasn't a soul in sight.

I ran and ran for miles, completely free. My legs didn't get tired, my lungs didn't burn. I felt like I could've kept going for days on end. I let out screams of joy that were more animalistic than human. At one point I jumped into the water and just floated, the ocean at my back and the soft drone of thousands of tiny splashes around me.

At that moment, I recalled how I felt during that first run in Lisbon. It was the same, visceral emotion that can only be described as full liberation. The common thread between those two experiences? Remote work. Being remote allowed me to be in both Portugal and Mexico, working and traveling. Being remote allowed me to take off for a run in the middle of my day without some boss in an office hounding me. Being remote allowed my sovereignty to exist.

This is the point of remote work—to give you the chance to press pause again and again in your life, capturing these liberating moments of time. Your child's uncontrollable giggle as your dog licks their face. A cup of matcha (with oat milk) on a chilly morning as the sun peeks its head over a mountainous horizon. A moment of connection with a stranger whose language you don't speak, but whose smile and hand gestures you understand perfectly.

I don't know what these moments of liberation may be for you, but whatever they are, I want you to experience them as much as possible.

That was the point of this book. Not to give you some menial tactic or strategy about what to put in a bullet point on your résumé, but to arm you with the information and inspiration you need to manifest the existence you deserve.

So here you are, at the end. I've shown you all types of buttons you can press to land a remote job and given you a remote for *your* life (while drastically overusing this *remote* wordplay). What are you waiting for? It's time to stop dreaming about working remotely, and start making it a reality. Go ahead, I dare you. Press play.

ACKNOWLEDGMENTS

WHEN I FIRST STARTED WRITING THE OUTLINE OF THIS BOOK IN 2018, I had no idea what it was going to turn into. I don't think anyone writing their first book does. After a long hiatus and a pandemic that turned our world upside down, picking up the book again in 2021 with Scribe Media felt like a huge undertaking. From there to now, it took a whole hell of a lot of people involved to help bring it to life. When I decided to also run a Kickstarter campaign to support the pre-sale and offer creative rewards to my backers, I was taken aback by the generosity and interest in *Remote for Life*. I'm grateful to take a moment to celebrate with supporters from the project by immortalizing your name in my book forever. This experience would be nothing without you.

My sincerest thanks:

Safetywing
Insurgent Publishing
The Creative Fund by BackerKit
Sivan Aharon
Marc Förster Algás
Dee Baden
Roy Baladi
Ian Balina

Jake Bennett
Joseph Bibelhausen
Kyle Borcik
Alex Boyd
Dylan Brix
Ricardo Campos
Clint Carroll
Joan Carroll

Lindsay Carroll

Sara Carroll

Victor Chan

Tiffany Cheung

John Cochran III

Mitchell Cohen

Jerald Crowser

Craig Dacy

Weston Davis

Andrew Desmarais

Alan Duro

Charles Egan

Cy Englert

Hallie Exall

Nicole Fernandez-Valle

Erica Forrence

Joshua Foster

Jessica Fuller

David Gauthier

Juan Pablo Besa González

Lumin Grace

Joseph Grinstain

Alexander Gross

Olivia Gulsvig

Sarah Hawley

Kevin Heaney

Andre Hinojosa

Rebecca Pate Huff

Brandon Jackson

Taylor Jacobson

Nicholas Jaeger

Jordan Jenkins

Mack Jenkins

Kumar Jerath

Mitko Karshovski

Kevin Koepsel

Scott Kozak

Gabe Krebs

Dean Kuchel

Alex Kunz

Nathan Kvalheim

Brittany Lopez Lewis

Brandon Loschiavo

James Lyon

Gianni Macri

Madeline Mann

Chris McCahill

Katelyn McCarthy

William McIlroy

Nicole Meloni

Tom Morkes

Jarrett Nixon

Benny B. Nobre

Brandon Pack

Jeremy W. Pease

Diana Perez

Artem Polyvyanny

Robin Austin Reed

Chris Reynolds

Matt Rodriguez

Ruben Rosado

Sergio Sala

Tyler Sellhorn

Matthew Sherman

Lise Slimane

Miles Spafford

Karen Stephen

Andrea Sofia

Danielle Tait

Faith Tallchief-Underwood

Brittany Thomas

Donata Tortella

Dominic Trovato

Nick Velardi

Michael Vincent

Jay Virdee

Katie Wallace

Chase Warrington

Ken Weary

Serge Zhevelyuk

Orest Zub

DOIST

WHAT WE DO

Founded in 2007, Doist is a pioneer of remote work that specializes in productivity software. We created the award-winning task management app Todoist and Twist, the first communication app designed for async workflows. Collectively, Doist supports twenty-five million people globally to stay organized and productive.

OUR MISSION

Our mission is to create a future where anyone can work hard and without distractions from anywhere in the world. Our core values are independence, mastery, communication, ambition & balance, and impact. They are few, but they are mighty. From creating processes to decision-making and recruiting, we build our five core values into nearly every single thing we do. By using our core values to model our behavior, we show the world that a more fulfilling future of work is possible-and is already happening.

HOW WE WORK REMOTELY

At Doist, we're constantly experimenting with ways to foster human connection in an async-first workplace. We're committed to building a company and culture with a lasting impact on the world. The conversation around remote work is quickly shifting from "How do we make this work right now?" to "How do we optimize remote work for the long term?" Team leaders are no longer satisfied with the immediate productivity benefits of remote work. They're now shifting the focus to building relationships with colleagues at a distance, promoting team camaraderie, and cultivating organizational culture-those vital elements of any team that exist outside the confines of KPIs and OKRs. It's a refreshing change.

doist.com

REMOTE COMPANY

REMOTE

WHAT WE DO

Remote creates software that makes it possible for companies to hire anyone from anywhere. We offer international payroll, benefits, taxes, and compliance for businesses big and small, whether it's in countries where they don't have entities or to manage and pay international contractors. Through our secure platform, we enable companies to pay in local currencies with zero exchange fees, manage all employment documents in one place, and offer tailored support for each country they want to hire in.

OUR MISSION

Talent is everywhere-opportunity is not. We're on a mission to open up the world of work for every person, business, and country. We have operationalized our values, and we use these in everything we do day to day. Our core values are excellence, kindness, ownership, transparency, and ambition.

HOW WE WORK REMOTELY

Remote is a global company. We do not have an office anywhere in the world. We are also not a corporate or traditional company whatsoever. We are a modern tech and product tech company with a people-first approach. Our entire team works remotely in countries around the world. We're passionate about what a game-changer it is to have that freedom. It also attracts more talented, diverse, and interesting people to our growing company!

remote.com

Featured

REMOTE COMPANY

TIME DOCTOR

WHAT WE DO

Time Doctor is a time tracking software company that provides actionable data and clear direction on how to improve performance and increase productivity so that teams become better each and every second. The aim of our software is to reduce time spent on distractions, help improve business processes by analyzing where time is spent, and help remote companies maintain a high level of productivity. We are the Fitbit for work.

OUR MISSION

Our mission is to empower the transition to remote work. This feeds into every major decision we make as a company. If something doesn't help the world transition to remote work, we don't do it. We believe that by measuring all of the data inside an organization openly and honestly, we can become better workers, partners, parents, and individuals. Our core values consist of statements about who we are. We are remote work advocates, passionate about what we do, determined, adaptable, and generous.

HOW WE WORK REMOTELY

We work asynchronously as much as possible. Employees at Time Doctor spend about 10% of their workday communicating synchronously. The other 90% is asynchronously. We measure this with our own tools. In addition, every Monday morning, everyone has a meeting with themselves to evaluate how they are exploring the company values in their own way and advocating for remote work.

timedoctor.com

Made in United States
Troutdale, OR
11/29/2023

15131230R00152